FREEDOM
OF THE PRESS

Other books in this series:

The Bill of Rights

FREEDOM
OF THE PRESS

Edited by David L. Hebert

Bruce Glassman, *Vice President*
Bonnie Szumski, *Publisher*
Helen Cothran, *Managing Editor*
Scott Barbour, *Series Editor*

GREENHAVEN PRESS
An imprint of Thomson Gale, a part of The Thomson Corporation

THOMSON
GALE

Detroit • New York • San Francisco • San Diego • New Haven, Conn.
Waterville, Maine • London • Munich

Cover credit: © Bettmann/CORBIS. A cameraman films the courtroom as the first degree murder trial of Dr. Samuel Sheppard gets under way.

LIBRARY OF CONGRESS CATALOGING-IN-PUBLICATION DATA

Freedom of the press / David L. Hebert, book editor.
    p. cm. — (The Bill of Rights)
Includes bibliographical references and index.
ISBN 0-7377-2047-6 (lib. : alk. paper)
    1. Freedom of the press—United States. 2. Freedom of the press—History.
I. Hebert, David L. II. The Bill of Rights (San Diego, Calif.)

KF4774.F73 2005
342.7308'53—dc22   2004054293

CONTENTS

Chapter 2: The Supreme Court and the Press in the Twentieth Century

"I cannot agree with those who think of the Bill of Rights as an 18th Century straightjacket, unsuited for this age. . . . The evils it guards against are not only old, they are with us now, they exist today."
—Hugo Black, associate justice of the
U.S. Supreme Court, 1937–1971

The Bill of Rights codifies the freedoms most essential to American democracy. Freedom of speech, freedom of religion, the right to bear arms, the right to a trial by a jury of one's peers, the right to be free from cruel and unusual punishment—these are just a few of the liberties that the Founding Fathers thought it necessary to spell out in the first ten amendments to the U.S. Constitution.

While the document itself is quite short (consisting of fewer than five hundred words), and while the liberties it protects often seem straightforward, the Bill of Rights has been a source of debate ever since its creation. Throughout American history, the rights the document protects have been tested and reinterpreted. Again and again, individuals perceiving violations of their rights have sought redress in the courts. The courts in turn have struggled to decipher the original intent of the founders as well as the need to accommodate changing societal norms and values.

The ultimate responsibility for addressing these claims has fallen to the U.S. Supreme Court. As the highest court in the nation, it is the Supreme Court's role to interpret the Constitution. The Court has considered numerous cases in which people have accused government of impinging on their rights. In the process, the Court has established a body of case law and precedents that have, in a sense, defined the Bill of Rights. In doing so, the Court has often reversed itself and introduced new ideas and approaches that have altered the legal meaning of the rights contained in the Bill of Rights. As a general rule, the Court has erred on the side of caution, upholding and expanding the rights of individuals rather than restricting them.

An example of this trend is the definition of cruel and unusual punishment. The Eighth Amendment specifically states, "Excessive bail shall not be required, nor excessive fines imposed, nor cruel and unusual punishments inflicted." However, over the years the Court has had to grapple with defining what constitutes "cruel and unusual punishment." In colonial America, punishments for crimes included branding, the lopping off of ears, and whipping. Indeed, these punishments were considered lawful at the time the Bill of Rights was written. Obviously, none of these punishments are legal today. In order to justify outlawing certain types of punishment that are deemed repugnant by the majority of citizens, the Court has ruled that it must consider the prevailing opinion of the masses when making such decisions. In overturning the punishment of a man stripped of his citizenship, the Court stated in 1958 that it must rely on society's "evolving standards of decency" when determining what constitutes cruel and unusual punishment. Thus the definition of cruel and unusual is not frozen to include only the types of punishment that were illegal at the time of the framing of the Bill of Rights; specific modes of punishment can be rejected as society deems them unjust.

Another way that the Courts have interpreted the Bill of Rights to expand individual liberties is through the process of "incorporation." Prior to the passage of the Fourteenth Amendment, the Bill of Rights was thought to prevent only the federal government from infringing on the rights listed in the document. However, the Fourteenth Amendment, which was passed in the wake of the Civil War, includes the words, ". . . nor shall any state deprive any person of life, liberty, or property, without due process of law; nor deny to any person within its jurisdiction the equal protection of the laws." Citing this passage, the Court has ruled that many of the liberties contained in the Bill of Rights apply to state and local governments as well as the federal government. This process of incorporation laid the legal foundation for the civil rights movement—most specifically the 1954 *Brown v. Board of Education* ruling that put an end to legalized segregation.

As these examples reveal, the Bill of Rights is not static. It truly is a living document that is constantly being reinterpreted and redefined. The Bill of Rights series captures this vital aspect of one of America's most cherished founding texts. Each volume in the series focuses on one particular right protected in the Bill of Rights. Through the use of primary and secondary sources, the right's evolution is traced from colonial times to the present. Primary sources include landmark Supreme Court rulings, speeches by prominent experts, and editorials. Secondary sources include historical analyses, law journal articles, book excerpts, and magazine articles. Each book also includes several features to facilitate research, including a bibliography, an annotated table of contents, an annotated list of relevant Supreme Court cases, an introduction, and an index. These elements help to make the Bill of Rights series a fascinating and useful tool for examining the fundamental liberties of American democracy.

During the colonial era in America, the British monarchy imposed restrictions on the press, dictating what could be published and brought to the attention of the public. This censorship was done by giving licenses to printers and publishers, which could easily be revoked if the publishers did not follow the rules dictated by the rulers of the time. The framers of the Constitution of the United States recognized that the press has an important role to play in keeping the public informed. Indeed, a free press was seen as an important safeguard against government tyranny. For this reason, they included press freedom in the First Amendment of the U.S. Constitution, which states in part, "Congress shall make no law . . . abridging the freedom of speech, or of the press." However, while freedom of the press is now guaranteed, the scope of the right is not clearly defined. It has been the job of scholars, philosophers, and judges to determine what the right actually encompasses. The ultimate challenge of defining these rights has fallen upon the Supreme Court.

The Court throughout history has frequently overturned state and federal laws that threatened constitutional rights —including the right to a free press. However, the Court has also determined that press freedom is not absolute and that some limitations on the press are necessary and justified. In various cases the Court has ruled that press rights can be curtailed. Two justifications the Court has cited for limiting the right of the press are the need to protect competing constitutional rights and to ensure national security.

Balancing Competing Rights

The rights guaranteed in the Constitution sometimes conflict with each other. It is the Court's duty in such situations to determine which right should receive greater emphasis. For example, a person accused of a criminal act has a number of rights—the right to a fair trial with a jury of one's peers, the right to face one's accuser, and the right to due process of law. However, the press also has the right to gather and disseminate information about the crime and the accused —activities that could potentially infringe on the defendant's rights.

A clash between press rights and a defendant's rights was considered in the 1966 case of *Sheppard v. Maxwell*. In 1954 Sam Sheppard had been convicted of murdering his wife. He appealed his conviction on the ground that he had not received a fair trial due to intense media coverage. The Court agreed that Sheppard's rights had been violated by excessive press involvement in the courtroom. The Court ruled that although the public has a right to know about court proceedings, a person accused of a crime also has the right to make a full and complete defense without outside interference from the press or other media influences. It is the trial court's job to ensure that if a constitutional right is to be infringed, the infringement must be as minimal as possible.

National Security

In addition to cases that have impacted individual rights, the Supreme Court has also reviewed cases in which the press has been restricted in order to protect the national security. In these instances, the government has argued that if certain information were released to the public via the press, the security of the country would be threatened.

One such case occurred in 1971, when reporters obtained some leaked documents that pertained to the Vietnam War and began to publish articles based on them. The documents were part of the Pentagon Papers, a seven-thousand-page top secret report that revealed government deception regarding the war. In the case that eventually became known as the Pentagon Papers case, the Supreme Court had to determine whether the release of the documents posed a genuine threat to national security, thereby justifying their suppression. The Court held that the government could not stop the publication of information unless it could be proven that dire consequences would result from the release of the information. In that particular case, the government could not meet the burden, and the documents were published.

National Security After September 11

After the events of the September 11, 2001, terrorist attacks on the United States, the government has faced a challenging task in trying to protect the nation against further attacks, as it must do so within the confines of the Constitution. The government must strike a delicate balance in trying to enact new laws that will protect the country but that will also protect individual rights. One law that has generated a great deal of debate is the Patriot Act, which grants broad powers to the FBI in obtaining secret wiretaps and conducting surveillance in the fight against terrorism.

The Patriot Act allows the FBI to obtain warrants that allow them to seize documents and records much more easily than was possible in the past, and even allows the warrants to be served upon people the government knows to be totally innocent. In addition, the act prohibits anyone from disclosing that the FBI has obtained the information, with criminal consequences if anyone breaches the prohibition. This act is viewed by many as a violation of the First Amendment as it impacts directly on the ability to publish information pertaining to government activities, although the issue has not yet come before the courts

Another free press issue related to the war on terror is the Pentagon's decision to "embed" reporters with active, frontline army units, where the reporters eat, sleep, drink, and maneuver with the troops. This process allowed for firsthand reporting of the conflicts in the 2003 Iraq War. It allowed the American people, for the first time, to actually experience the frontline warfare as it unfolded in real time, rather than having to wait for the newspapers or correspondents' reports as they did in prior conflicts.

The process, however, has come under fire. Critics say that participating journalists are unable to keep their reports impartial and objective. Others argue that the military is allowed too much control in establishing what information the reporters may and may not report. The objective of including the press on the front lines is noble; it provides the public with immediate knowledge of the actions of the troops overseas. However, it remains to be seen whether the military's control over the release of information constitutes a violation of free press rights.

Keeping Government Accountable

The constitutional guarantee of press freedom is important because it ensures that the public has access to information about its country and its government. It helps the people ensure that the government is accountable. However, press freedom is not absolute. The guarantee must continue to be evaluated against other competing rights, such as the rights of an accused in the court process and the right of the government to protect national security. In the end, the courts must continue to balance these competing interests.

CHAPTER ONE

The Early History of Freedom of the Press

The Bill of Rights

Freedom of the Press in Eighteenth-Century England

David Hume

Prior to 1776 the colonies were governed by the English common law. After the signing of the Declaration of Independence, much of this common law was incorporated into the laws of the new states. Part of that law included the lengths to which the press could be regulated or restrained. In the following excerpt, published in 1742, David Hume, a Scottish professor of philosophy, describes the status of freedom of the press in the United Kingdom. He contends that freedom of the press is the result of Britain's mixed form of government, which is part republican and part monarchical. The free press is necessary in order to preserve the republican aspect of the government from abuse of power on the part of the monarchy. These basic principles would later form the foundation for the adoption of the First Amendment and its guarantee of freedom of the press in the United States.

Nothing is more apt to surprise a foreigner than the extreme liberty which we enjoy in this country of communicating whatever we please to the public and of openly censuring every measure entered into by the king or his ministers. If the administration resolve upon war, it is affirmed that, either willfully or ignorantly, they mistake the interests of the nation; and that peace, in the present situation of affairs, is infinitely preferable. If the passion of the ministers lie toward peace, our political writers breathe nothing but war and devastation, and represent the specific conduct of the government as mean and pusillanimous. As this liberty is not indulged in any other government, either republican

David Hume, "Of the Liberty of the Press," *Essays Moral, Political, and Literary,* 1742.

or monarchical—in Holland and Venice more than in France or Spain—it may very naturally give occasion to the question: *How it happens that Great Britain alone enjoys this peculiar privilege?* And whether the unlimited exercise of this liberty be advantageous or prejudicial to the public.

The reason why the laws indulge us in such a liberty seems to be derived from our mixed form of government, which is neither wholly monarchical nor wholly republican. It will be found, if I mistake not, a true observation in politics that the two extremes in government, liberty and slavery, commonly approach nearest to each other; and that, as you depart from the extremes and mix a little of monarchy with liberty, the government becomes always the more free, and on the other hand, when you mix a little of liberty with monarchy, the yoke becomes always the more grievous and intolerable. In a government, such as that of France, which is absolute and where law, custom, and religion concur, all of them, to make the people fully satisfied with their condition, the monarch cannot entertain any *jealousy* against his subjects and therefore is apt to indulge them in great *liberties*, both of speech and action. In a government altogether republican, such as that of Holland, where there is no magistrate so eminent as to give *jealousy* to the state, there is no danger in entrusting the magistrates with large discretionary powers; and though many advantages result from such powers, in preserving peace and order, yet they lay a considerable restraint on men's actions and make every private citizen pay a great respect to the government. Thus it seems evident that the two extremes of absolute monarchy and of a republic approach near to each other in some material circumstances. In the *first* the magistrate has no jealousy of the people, in the *second* the people have none of the magistrate; which want of jealousy begets a mutual confidence and trust in both cases and produces a species of liberty in monarchies and of arbitrary power in republics. . . .

The Certainty of the Rule of Law

As the republican part of the government prevails in England, though with a great mixture of monarchy, it is obliged, for its own preservation, to maintain a watchful *jealousy* over the magistrates, to remove all discretionary powers, and to secure everyone's life and fortune by general and inflexible laws. No action must be deemed a crime but what the law has plainly determined to be such; no crime must be imputed to a man but from a legal proof before his judges, and even these judges must be his fellow subjects, who are obliged by their own interest to have a watchful eye over the encroachments and violence of the ministers. From these causes it proceeds that there is as much liberty, and even perhaps licentiousness, in Great Britain as there were formerly slavery and tyranny in Rome.

These principles account for the great liberty of the press in these kingdoms beyond what is indulged in any other government. It is apprehended that arbitrary power would steal in upon us were we not careful to prevent its progress and were there not an easy method of conveying the alarm from one end of the kingdom to the other. The spirit of the people must frequently be roused in order to curb the ambition of the court, and the dread of rousing this spirit must be employed to prevent that ambition. Nothing so effectual to this purpose as the liberty of the press, by which all the learning, wit, and genius of the nation may be employed on the side of freedom and everyone be animated to its defense. As long, therefore, as the republican part of our government can maintain itself against the monarchical, it will naturally be careful to keep the press open, as of importance to its own preservation.

A Common Right of Mankind

Since, therefore, the liberty of the press is so essential to the support of our mixed government, this sufficiently decides the second question: *Whether this liberty be advantageous or prejudicial*, there being nothing of greater importance in every state than the preservation of the ancient government, especially if it be a free one. But I would fain go a step further and assert that such a liberty is attended with so few inconveniences that it may be claimed as the common right of mankind and ought to be indulged them almost in every government except the ecclesiastical, to which, indeed, it would be fatal. We need not dread from this liberty any such ill consequences as followed from the harangues of the popular demagogues of Athens and tribunes of Rome. A man reads a book or pamphlet alone and coolly. There is none present from whom he can catch the passion by contagion. He is not hurried away by the force and energy of action. And should he be wrought up to never so seditious a humor, there is no violent resolution presented to him by which he can immediately vent his passion. The liberty of the press, therefore, however abused, can scarce ever excite popular tumults or rebellion. And as to those murmurs or secret discontents it may occasion, it is better they should get vent in words, that they may come to the knowledge of the magistrate before it be too late, in order to his providing a remedy against them. Mankind, it is true, have always a greater propension to believe what is said to the disadvantage of their governors than the contrary; but this inclination is inseparable from them whether they have liberty or not. A whisper may fly as quick and be as pernicious as a pamphlet. Nay, it will be more pernicious where men are not accustomed to think freely or distinguish betwixt truth and falsehood. . . .

It is a very comfortable reflection to the lovers of liberty that this peculiar privilege of *Britain* is of a kind that cannot easily be wrested from us and must last as long as our government remains in any degree free and independent. It is seldom that liberty of any kind is lost all at once. Slavery has so frightful an aspect to men accustomed to freedom that it must steal in upon them by degrees and must disguise itself in a thousand shapes in order to be received. But if the liberty of the press ever be lost, it must be lost at once. The general laws against sedition and libeling are at present as strong as they possibly can be made. Nothing can impose a further restraint but either the clapping an imprimatur upon the press or the giving very large discretionary powers to the court to punish whatever displeases them. But these concessions would be such a barefaced violation of liberty that they will probably be the last efforts of a despotic government. We may conclude that the liberty of *Britain* is gone forever when these attempts shall succeed.

An Early Defense of Press Freedom in Colonial America

Andrew Hamilton

John Peter Zenger, a publisher in early eighteenth-century America, printed some material in his *New York Weekly Journal* that criticized the governor of the colony. Zenger was charged with seditious libel. The law of record at the time was that an accused could be convicted of seditious libel even if the printed statements were true. Andrew Hamilton, an eminent attorney, argued the case for Zenger. In the following excerpt from his summation before the court, Hamilton argues that freedom to complain about an official's abuse of power is necessary in order to preserve liberty. Therefore, true statements about government officials should not be considered libel. Hamilton successfully convinced the jury not to convict, thus establishing a long-standing precedent in U.S. law: Truth is a valid defense against a charge of libel.

May it please Your Honor [James Delancey, chief justice of the province of New York], I was saying that notwithstanding all the duty and reverence claimed by Mr. Attorney [prosecutor Richard Bradley, attorney general of the king for the province of New York] to men in authority, they are not exempt from observing the rules of common justice either in their private or public capacities. The laws of our mother country know no exemptions. It is true that men in power are harder to be come at for wrongs they do either to a private person or to the public, especially a governor in The Plantations, where they insist upon an exemption from answering complaints of any kind in their own government. We are indeed told, and it is true, that they are obliged to answer

Andrew Hamilton, summation in the trial of John Peter Zenger, 1735.

a suit in the king's courts at Westminster for a wrong done to any person here. But do we not know how impracticable this is to most men among us, to leave their families, who depend upon their labor and care for their livelihood, and carry evidence to Britain, and at a great, nay, a far greater expense than almost any of us are able to bear, only to prosecute a governor for an injury done here?

But when the oppression is general, there is no remedy even that way. No, our Constitution has—blessed be God—given us an opportunity, if not to have such wrongs redressed, yet by our prudence and resolution we may in a great measure prevent the committing of such wrongs by making a governor sensible that it is in his interest to be just to those under his care. For such is the sense that men in general—I mean free men—have of common justice, that when they come to know that a chief magistrate abuses the power with which he is trusted for the good of the people, and is attempting to turn that very power against the innocent, whether of high or low degree, I say that mankind in general seldom fail to interpose, and, as far as they can, prevent the destruction of their fellow subjects.

And has it not often been seen—I hope it will always be seen that when the representatives of a free people are by just representations or remonstrances made sensible of the sufferings of their fellow subjects, by the abuse of power in the hands of a governor, that they have declared (and loudly too) that they were not obliged by any law to support a governor who goes about to destroy a Province or Colony, or their privileges, which by His Majesty he was appointed, and by the law he is bound, to protect and encourage? But I pray that it may be considered—of what use is this mighty privilege if every man that suffers is silent? And if a man must be taken up as a libeler for telling his sufferings to his neighbor?

I know that it may be answered, "Have you not a legislature? Have you not a House of Representatives to whom you may complain?" To this I answer, "We have." But what then? Is an Assembly to be troubled with every injury done by a governor? Or are they to hear of nothing but what those in the administration will please to tell them? And what sort of trial must a man have? How is he to be remedied, especially if the case were, as I have known to happen in America in my time, that a governor who has places—I will not say pensions, for I believe they seldom give that to another which they can take to themselves—to bestow can keep the same Assembly, after he has modeled them so as to get a majority of the House in his interest, for near twice seven years together? I pray, what redress is to be expected for an honest man who makes his complaint against a governor to an Assembly who may properly enough be said to be made by the same governor against whom the complaint is made? The thing answers itself.

Men Are Entitled to Complain

No, it is natural, it is a privilege, I will go farther, it is a right, which all free men claim, that they are entitled to complain when they are hurt. They have a right publicly to remonstrate against the abuses of power in the strongest terms, to put their neighbors upon their guard against the craft or open violence of men in authority, and to assert with courage the sense they have of the blessings of liberty, the value they put upon it, and their resolution at all hazards to preserve it as one of the greatest blessings heaven can bestow.

When a House of Assembly composed of honest freemen sees the general bent of the people's inclination, that is which it must and will, I am sure it ought to, weigh with a legislature in spite of all the craft, caressing, and cajoling made use of by a governor to divert them from harkening to the voice of their country. As we all very well understand the true reason why gentlemen take so much pains and make such great interest to be appointed governors, so is the design of their appointment not less manifest. We know His Majesty's gracious intentions toward his subjects. He desires no more than that his people in The Plantations should be kept up to their duty and allegiance to the crown of Great Britain, that peace may be preserved among them, and justice impartially administered; so that we may be governed so as to render us useful to our mother country by encouraging us to make and raise such commodities as may be useful to Great Britain.

But will anyone say that all or any of these good ends are to be effected by a governor's setting his people together by the ears, and by the assistance of one part of the people to plague and plunder the other? The commission that governors bear while they execute the powers given them according to the intent of the royal grantor requires and deserves very great reverence and submission. But when a governor departs from the duty enjoined on him by his sovereign, and acts as if he were less accountable than the royal hand that gave him all that power and honor that he is possessed of, this sets people upon examining and inquiring into the power, authority, and duty of such a magistrate, and to comparing those with his conduct. And just as far as they find he exceeds the bounds of his authority, or falls short in doing impartial justice to the people under his administration, so far they very often, in return, come short in their duty to such a governor.

For power alone will not make a man beloved, and I have heard it observed that the man who was neither good nor wise before his being made a governor never mended upon his preferment, but has been generally observed to be worse. For men who are not imbued with wisdom and virtue can only be kept in bounds by the law; and by how much the further they think themselves out of the reach of the law, by so much the more wicked and cruel men are. I wish there were no instances of the kind at this day.

Wherever this happens to be the case of a governor, unhappy are the people under his administration, and in the end he will find himself so too, for the people will neither love him nor support him. . . .

Only False Complaints Can Be Restricted

But to proceed. I beg leave to insist that the right of complaining or remonstrating is natural; that the restraint upon this natural right is the law only; and that those restraints can only extend to what is false. For as it is truth alone that can excuse or justify any man for complaining of a bad administration, I as frankly agree that nothing ought to excuse a man who raises a false charge or accusation even against a private person, and that no manner of allowance ought to be made to him who does so against a public magistrate.

Truth ought to govern the whole affair of libels. And yet the party accused runs risk enough even then; for if he fails in proving every tittle of what he has written, and to the satisfaction of the court and jury too, he may find to his cost that when the prosecution is set on foot by men in power it seldom wants friends to favor it. . . .

There is heresy in law as well as in religion, and both have changed very much. We well know that it is not two centuries ago that a man would have been burned as a heretic for owning such opinions in matters of religion as are publicly written and printed at this day. They were fallible men, it seems, and we take the liberty not only to differ from them in religious opinions, but to condemn them and their opinions too. I must presume that in taking these freedoms in thinking and speaking about matters of faith or religion, we are in the right; for although it is said that there are very great liberties of this kind taken in New York, yet I have heard of no information preferred by Mr. Attorney for any offenses of this sort. From which I think it is pretty clear that in New York a man may make very free with his God, but he must take a special care what he says of his governor.

It is agreed upon by all men that this is a rein of liberty. While men keep within the bounds of truth I hope they may with safety both speak and write their sentiments of the conduct of men in power, I mean of that part of their conduct only which affects the liberty or property of the people under their administration. Were this to be denied, then the next step may make them slaves; for what notions can be entertained of slavery beyond that of suffering the greatest injuries and oppressions without the liberty of complaining, or if they do, to be destroyed, body and estate, for so doing?

Abuse of Power

It is said and insisted on by Mr. Attorney that government is a sacred thing; that it is to be supported and reverenced; that it is government that protects our persons and estates, prevents treasons, murders, robberies, riots, and all the train of evils that overturns kingdoms and states and ruins particular persons. And if those in the administration, especially the supreme magistrate, must have all their conduct censured by private men, government cannot subsist. This is called a licentiousness not to be tolerated. It is said that it brings the rulers of the people into contempt, and their authority not to be regarded, and so in the end the laws cannot be put into execution.

These, I say, and such as these, are the general topics insisted upon by men in power and their advocates. But I wish it might be considered at the same time how often it has happened that the abuse of power has been the primary cause of these evils, and that it was the injustice and oppression of these great men that has commonly brought them into contempt with the people. The craft and art of such men is great, and who that is the least acquainted with history or law can be ignorant of the specious pretenses that have often been made use of by men in power to introduce arbitrary rule, and to destroy the liberties of a free people?

This is the second information for libeling of a governor that I have known in America. The first, although it may look like a romance, yet as it is true I will beg leave to mention it.

Governor Nicholson, who happened to be offended with one of his clergy, met him one day upon the road; and as usual with him (under the protection of his commission) used the poor parson with the worst of language, and threatened to cut off his ears, slit his nose, and at last to shoot him through the head. The parson, being a reverend man, continued all this time uncovered in the heat of the sun, until he found an opportunity to fly for it. Coming to a neighbor's house, he felt himself very ill of a fever, and immediately writes for a doctor. And that his physician might the better judge of his distemper, he acquainted him with the usage he had received; concluding that the Governor was certainly mad, for that no man in his senses would have behaved in that manner.

The doctor unhappily showed the parson's letter. The Governor came to hear of it. And so an information was preferred against the poor man for saying he believed the Governor was mad. It was laid down in the information to be false, scandalous, and wicked, and written with intent to move sedition among the people, and to bring His Excellency into contempt. But by an order from the late Queen Anne there was a stop put to that prosecution, with sundry others set on foot by the same Governor against gentlemen of the greatest worth and honor in that government.

Everything Is Libel

And may not I be allowed, after all this, to say that by a little countenance almost anything that a man writes may, with the help of that useful term of art called an innuendo be construed to be a libel, according to Mr. Attorney's definition of it—to wit, that whether the words are spoken of a person of a public character or of a private man, whether dead or living, good or bad, true or false, all make a libel. For according to Mr. Attorney, after a man hears a writing read, or reads and repeats it, or laughs at it, they are all punishable. It is true that Mr. Attorney is so good as to allow it must be after the party knows it to be a libel, but he is not so kind as to take the man's word for it.

If a libel is understood in the large and unlimited sense urged by Mr. Attorney, there is scarce a writing I know that may not be called a libel, or scarce a person safe from being called to an account as a libeler. For Moses, meek as he was, libeled Cain; and who is it that has not libeled the Devil?

For according to Mr. Attorney it is no justification to say that one has a bad name. . . . How must a man speak or write; or what must he hear, read, or sing; or when must he laugh so as to be secure from being taken up as a libeler?

The Risk of Presuming Innuendo

I sincerely believe that were some persons to go through the streets of New York nowadays and read a part of the Bible, if it was not known to be such, Mr. Attorney, with the help of his innuendos, would easily turn it into a libel. As for instance Isaiah 9:16: "The leaders of the people cause them to err; and they that are led by them are destroyed." Should Mr. Attorney go about to make this a libel, he would read it thus: "The leaders of the people (innuendo, the Governor and Council of New York) cause them (innuendo, the people of this Province) to err, and they (the people of this Province meaning) that are led by them (the Governor and Council meaning) are destroyed (innuendo, are deceived into the loss of their liberty), which is the worst kind of destruction."

Or if some person should publicly repeat, in a manner not pleasing to his betters, the fourth and fifth verses of the 56th chapter of the same book, there Mr. Attorney would have a large field to display his skill in the artful application of his innuendos. The words are: "His watchmen are blind, they are all ignorant. . . . Yea, they are greedy dogs which can never have enough." To make them a libel there is, according to Mr. Attorney's doctrine, no more wanting but the aid of his skill in the right adapting of his innuendos. As for instance: "His watchmen (innuendo, the Governors Council and his Assembly) are blind, they are all ignorant (innuendo, will not see the dangerous designs of His Excellency). Yea, they (the Governor and Council meaning) are greedy dogs which can never have enough (innuendo, enough of riches and power)."

Such an instance as this seems only fit to be laughed at; but I appeal to Mr. Attorney himself whether these are not at least equally proper to be applied to His Excellency and his ministers as some of the inferences and innuendos in his information against my client. Then if Mr. Attorney is at liberty to come into court and file an information in the king's name, without leave, who is secure whom he is pleased to prosecute as a libeler?

And give me leave to say that the mode of prosecuting by information, when a grand jury will not find a true bill, is a national grievance, and greatly inconsistent with that freedom that the subjects of England enjoy in most other cases. But if we are so unhappy as not to be able to ward off this stroke of power directly, yet let us take care not to be cheated out of our liberties by forms and appearances. Let us always be sure that the charge in the information is made out clearly even beyond a doubt; for although matters in the information may be called form upon trial, yet they may be, and often have been found to be, matters of substance upon giving judgment.

Gentlemen: The danger is great in proportion to the mischief that may happen through our too great credulity. A proper confidence in a court is commendable, but as the verdict, whatever it is, will be yours, you ought to refer no part of your duty to the discretion of other persons. If you should be of the opinion that there is no falsehood in Mr. Zenger's papers, you will, nay pardon me for the expression, you ought, to say so—because you do not know whether others—I mean the Court—may be of that opinion. It is your right to do so, and there is much depending upon your resolution as well as upon your integrity. The loss of liberty, to a generous mind, is worse than death. And yet we know that there have been those in all ages who for the sake of preferment, or some imaginary honor, have freely lent a helping hand to oppress, nay to destroy, their country. . . .

The Danger of Power

Power may justly be compared to a great river. While kept within its due bounds it is both beautiful and useful. But when it overflows its banks, it is then too impetuous to be stemmed; it bears down all before it, and brings destruction and desolation wherever it comes. If, then, this is the nature of power, let us at least do our duty, and like wise men who value freedom use our utmost care to support liberty, the only bulwark against lawless power, which in all ages has sacrificed to its wild lust and boundless ambition the blood of the best men that ever lived.

I hope to be pardoned, Sir, for my zeal upon this occasion. It is an old and wise caution that when our neighbor's house is on fire we ought to take care of our own. For though—blessed be God I live in a government where liberty is well understood and freely enjoyed, yet experience has shown us all—I am sure it has to me that a bad precedent in one government is soon set up for an authority in another. And therefore I cannot but think it my, and every honest man's duty, that while we pay all due obedience to men in authority we ought at the same time to be upon our guard against power wherever we apprehend that it may affect ourselves or our fellow subjects.

I am truly very unequal to such an undertaking on many accounts. You see that I labor under the weight of many years, and am bowed down with great infirmities of body. Yet, old and weak as I am, I should think it my duty, if required, to go to the utmost part of the land where my services could be of any use in assisting to quench the flame of prosecutions upon informations, set on foot by the government to deprive a people of the right of remonstrating and complaining, too, of the arbitrary attempts of men in power.

Men who injure and oppress the people under their administration provoke them to cry out and complain, and then make that very complaint the foundation for new oppressions and prosecutions. I wish I could say that there were no instances of this kind.

But to conclude. The question before the Court and you, Gentlemen of the jury, is not of small or private concern. It is not the cause of one poor printer, nor of New York alone, which you are now trying. No! It may in its consequence affect every free man that lives under a British government on the main of America. It is the best cause. It is the cause of liberty. And I make no doubt but your upright conduct this day will not only entitle you to the love and esteem of your fellow citizens, but every man who prefers freedom to a life of slavery will bless and honor you as men who have baffled the attempt of tyranny, and by an impartial and uncorrupt verdict have laid a noble foundation for securing to ourselves, our posterity, and our neighbors, that to which nature and the laws of our country have given us a right to liberty of both exposing and opposing arbitrary power (in these parts of the world at least) by speaking and writing truth.

Defining Libel and Its Defenses

William Blackstone

William Blackstone was an eighteenth-century British lawyer, law professor, judge, politician, and scholar. His series of lectures at Oxford University on the common law later became one of the most revered legal references and influenced the framers of the U.S. Constitution in drafting their own document. The following excerpt from Blackstone's *Commentaries on the Laws of England* defines libel and its civil and criminal distinctions. In a civil case, the truth of the information published can be a defense against the action, but with criminal libel, no such defense exists. Blackstone also distinguishes between the concept of prior restraint, in which the government stops the press before publication, and the concept of libel, which provides a remedy for a person who has been wronged by the press. The law against libel, Blackstone contends, is required to ensure that the press remains free, but does not overstep its bounds by defaming people or inciting violence.

---

*L*ibels, *libelli famosi*, . . . taken in their largest and most extensive sense, signify any writings, pictures, or the like, of an immoral or illegal tendency; but, in the sense under which we are now to consider them, are malicious defamations of any person, and especially a magistrate, made public by either printing, writing, signs, or pictures, in order to provoke him to wrath, or expose him to public hatred, contempt, and ridicule. The direct tendency of these libels is the breach of the public peace, by stirring up the objects of them to revenge, and perhaps to bloodshed. The communication of a libel to any one person is a publication in the eye of the law: and therefore the sending an abusive private letter to a man

William Blackstone, *Commentaries on the Laws of England*, circa 1765–1769.

is as much a libel as if it were openly printed, for it equally tends to a breach of the peace. For the same reason it is immaterial with respect to the essence of a libel, whether the matter of it be true or false; since the provocation, and not the falsity, is the thing to be punished criminally: though, doubtless, the falsehood of it may aggravate its guilt, and enhance its punishment. In a civil action, we may remember, a libel must appear to be false, as well as scandalous; for, if the charge be true, the plaintiff has received no private injury, and has no ground to demand a compensation for himself, whatever offence it may be against the public peace: and therefore, upon a civil action, the truth of the accusation may be pleaded in bar of the suit. But, in a criminal prosecution, the tendency which all libels have to create animosities, and to disturb the public peace, is the sole consideration of the law. And therefore, in such prosecutions, the only facts to be considered are, first, the making or publishing of the book or writing; and secondly, whether the matter be criminal: and, if both these points are against the defendant, the offence against the public is complete. The punishment of such libellers, for either making, repeating, printing, or publishing the libel, is fine, and such corporal punishment as the court in their discretion shall inflict; regarding the quantity of the offence, and the quality of the offender. . . .

In this, and the other instances which we have lately considered, where blasphemous, immoral, treasonable, schismatical, seditious, or scandalous libels are punished by the English law, some with a greater, others with a less degree of severity; the *liberty of the press*, properly understood, is by no means infringed or violated. The liberty of the press is indeed essential to the nature of a free state: but this consists in laying no *previous* restraints upon publications, and not in freedom from censure for criminal matter when published. Every freeman has an undoubted right to lay what sentiments he pleases before the public: to forbid this, is to destroy the freedom of the press: but if he publishes what is improper, mischievous, or illegal, he must take the consequence of his own temerity. To subject the press to the restrictive power of a licenser, as was formerly done, both before and since the [English civil wars of

1638–1660], is to subject all freedom of sentiment to the prejudices of one man, and make him the arbitrary and infallible judge of all controverted points in learning, religion, and government. But to punish (as the law does at present) any dangerous or offensive writings, which, when published, shall on a fair and impartial trial be adjudged of a pernicious tendency, is necessary for the preservation of peace and good order, of government and religion, the only solid foundations of civil liberty. Thus the will of individuals is still left free; the abuse only of that free will is the object of legal punishment. Neither is any restraint hereby laid upon freedom of thought or enquiry: liberty of private sentiment is still left; the disseminating, or making public, of bad sentiments, destructive of the ends of society, is the crime which society corrects. A man (says a fine writer on this subject) may be allowed to keep poisons in his closet, but not publicly to vend them as cordials. And to this we may add, that the only plausible argument heretofore used for restraining the just freedom of the press, "that it was necessary to prevent the daily abuse of it," will entirely lose its force, when it is shewn (by a seasonable exertion of the laws) that the press cannot be abused to any bad purpose, without incurring a suitable punishment: whereas it never can be used to any good one, when under the control of an inspector. So true will it be found, that to censure the licentiousness, is to maintain the liberty, of the press.

Truth Becomes a Defense for Libel

James Kent

Once the First Amendment became ratified, a new constitutional right had been entrenched and became a part of the supreme law of the land. In the years following, much debate centered around the actual meaning of the "freedom of the press" and exactly what role the government could play in limiting the right to free speech. One of the most important factors at the time was the concept of libel, a common law remedy that allowed a person to sue the publisher of material that might seem harmful to that person's reputation. Further, a criminal element of libel also existed; a publisher could be charged criminally for "seditious libel"—writings that might incite riots or public uprisings.

In the early nineteenth century James Kent, a former justice of the New York Supreme Court, penned a lengthy and comprehensive treatise on the American law. In this excerpt, Kent provides an overview of the need to strike a balance between competing interests when determining the scope of the right of the freedom of the press. Specifically, he addresses the question of allowing defendants to argue the truthfulness of their statements as a defense against both criminal and civil charges of libel.

As a part of the right of personal security, the preservation of every person's good name from the vile arts of detraction is justly included. The laws of the ancients, no less than those of modern nations, made private reputation one of the objects of their protection. The Roman law took a just distinction between slander spoken and written; and the

James Kent, *Commentaries on American Law, Volume 1,* New York, 1826.

same distinction prevails in our law, which considers the slander of a private person by words, in no other light than a civil injury, for which a pecuniary compensation may be obtained. The injury consists in falsely and maliciously charging another with the commission of some public offence, or the breach of some public trust, or with any matter in relation to his particular trade or vocation, and which, if true, would render him unworthy of employment; or, lastly, with any other matter or thing, by which special injury is sustained. But if the slander be communicated by pictures, or signs, or writing, or printing, it is calculated to have a wider circulation, to make a deeper impression, and to become proportionably more injurious.

Expressions which tend to render a man ridiculous, or lower him in the esteem and opinion of the world, would be libellous if printed, though they would not be actionable if spoken. A libel, as applicable to individuals, has been well defined to be a malicious publication, expressed either in printing or writing, or by signs or pictures, tending either to blacken the memory of one dead, or the reputation of one alive, and expose him to public hatred, contempt, or ridicule. A malicious intent towards government, magistrates, or individuals, and an injurious or offensive tendency, must concur to constitute the libel. It then becomes a grievance, and the law has accordingly considered it in the light of a public as well as a private injury, and has rendered the party not only liable to a private suit at the instance of the party libelled, but answerable to the state by indictment, as guilty of an offence tending directly to a breach of the public peace.

Liberty of Speech and the Press

But though the law be solicitous to protect every man in his fair fame and character, it is equally careful that the liberty of speech, and of the press, should be duly preserved. The liberal communication of sentiment, and entire freedom of discussion, in respect to the character and conduct of public men, and of candidates for public favour, is deemed essential to the judicious exercise of the right of suffrage, and of that control over their rulers, which resides in the free people of these United States. It has, accordingly, become a constitutional principle in this country, that "every citizen may freely speak, write, and publish his sentiments, on all subjects, being responsible for the abuse of that right, and that no law can rightfully be passed to restrain or abridge the freedom of speech, or of the press."

The History of Libel Law

The law of England, even under the Anglo-Saxon line of princes, took severe and exemplary notice of defamation, as an offence against the public peace, and in the time of Henry III., [Henry de] Bracton [an English judge of the thirteenth century] adopted the language of the Institutes of [Roman emperor] Justinian, and held slander and libellous writings to be actionable injuries. But the first private suit for slanderous words to be met with in the English law, was in the reign of Edward III., and for the high offence of charging another with a crime which endangered his life. The mischiefs of licensed abuse were felt to be so extensive, and so incompatible with the preservation of peace, that several acts of parliament, known as the statutes *de scandalis magnatum* [of great scandal], were passed to suppress and punish the propagation of false and malicious slander. They are said to have been declaratory of the common law, and actions of slander were slowly, but gradually multiplied, between the time of Edward III., and the reign of Elizabeth, when they had become frequent. The remedy was applied to a variety of cases; and in a private action of slander for damages, and even in the action of *scandalum magnatum*, the defendant was allowed to justify, by showing the truth of the fact charged, for if the words were true, it was then a case of *damnum absque injuria* [a loss or damage not serious enough for the law to intervene], according to the just opinion of Paulus, in the civil law. But in the case of a public prosecution for a libel, it became the established principle of the English law, as declared in the Court of Star Chamber, about the beginning of the reign of James I. that the truth of the libel could not be shown by way of justification, because, whether true or false, it was equally dangerous to the public peace.

Truth Inadmissible as a Defence for Libel

The same doctrine remains in England to this day unshaken; and in the case of *The King v. Burdett*, it was held, that where a libel imputes to others the commission of a triable crime, the evidence of the truth of it was inadmissible, and that the intention was to be collected from the paper itself, unless explained by the mode of publication, or other circumstances, and that if the contents were likely to produce mischief, the defendant must be presumed to intend *that* which his act was likely to produce. "The liberty of the press," as one of the judges in that case observed, "cannot impute criminal conduct to others without violating the right of character, and that right can only be attacked in a court of justice, where the party attacked has a fair opportunity of defending himself. Where vituperation begins, the liberty of the press ends." Whether the rule of the English law was founded on a just basis, and whether it was applicable to the free press and free institutions in this country, has been a question extensively and laboriously discussed in several cases which have been brought before our American tribunals.

In the case of *The People v. Croswell*, which came before the Supreme Court of this state in 1804, and was argued at the bar with very great ability, the court were equally divided in opinion on the point, whether, on an indictment for a libel, the defendant was entitled to give in evidence to the jury the truth of the charges contained in the libel. In the Court of Appeals in South Carolina, in 1811, the court unanimously decided, in the case of *The State v. Lehre*, that by the English common law it was settled, on sound principles of policy derived from the civil law, that the defendant had no right to justify the libel by giving the truth of it in evidence. The court, in the learned and able opinion which was delivered in that case, considered that the law, as then declared, was not only the law of England, but probably the law of all Europe, and of most of the free states of America. The same question has been frequently discussed in Massachusetts. In the case of *The Commonwealth v. Chase*, in 1808, it was decided, that the publication of a libel maliciously, and with intent to defame, was clearly a public offence, whether the libel be true

or not; and the rule was held to be founded on sound principles, indispensable to restrain all tendencies to breaches of
the peace, and to private animosity and revenge. The essence
of the offence consisted in the malicious intent to defame the
reputation of another; and a man may maliciously publish
the truth against another with the intent to defame his character, and if the publication be true, the tendency of the publication to inflame the passions, and to excite revenge, is not
diminished. But though a defendant, on an indictment for a
libel, cannot justify himself for publishing the libel, merely
by proving the truth of it, yet he may repel the criminal
charge by proving that the publication was for a justifiable
purpose, and not malicious; and if the purpose be justifiable,
the defendant may give in evidence the truth of the words,
when such evidence will tend to negative the malicious intent to defame. The same question was again agitated and
discussed before the same court in 1825, in the case of *The
Commonwealth v. Blanding*, and the court strongly enforced
the doctrine of the former case, that, as a general rule, the
truth of the libel was not admissible in evidence upon the
trial of the indictment; and this principle of the common law
was declared to be founded in common sense and common
justice, and prevailed in the codes of every civilized country.
It was further held, that whether in any particular case such
evidence be admissible, was to be determined by the court;
and, if admissible, then the jury were to determine whether
the publication was made with good motives, and for justifiable ends. The same rule, that the truth cannot be admitted
in evidence on indictment for a libel, though it may in a civil
suit for damages, has been adjudged in Louisiana; and the
weight of judicial authority undoubtedly is, that the English
common law doctrine of libel is the common law doctrine in
this country, in all cases in which it has not been expressly
controlled by constitutional or legislative provisions. The decisions in Massachusetts and Louisiana were made notwithstanding the constitution of the one state had declared, that
"the liberty of the press ought not to be restrained," and that
the other had said, that "every citizen might freely speak,
write, and print, on any subject, being responsible for the

abuse of that liberty." Those decisions went only to control the malicious abuse or licentiousness of the press, and that is the most effectual way to preserve its freedom in the genuine sense of the constitutional declarations on the subject. Without such a check, the press, in the hands of evil and designing men, would become a most formidable engine, and as mighty for mischief as for good. Since the decision in 1825, the legislature of Massachusetts have interposed, and by an act passed in March, 1827, have allowed the truth to be given in evidence in all prosecutions for libels, but with a proviso that such evidence should not be a justification, unless it should be made satisfactorily to appear upon the trial, that the matter charged as libellous was published with good motives, and for justifiable ends.

A Movement Toward the Truth

The constitutions of several of the United States have made special provision in favour of giving the truth in evidence in public prosecutions for libels. In the constitutions of Pennsylvania, Delaware, Tennessee, Kentucky, Ohio, Indiana, and Illinois, it is declared, that in prosecutions for libels on men in respect to their public official conduct, the truth may be given in evidence, when the matter published was proper for public information. In the constitutions of Mississippi and Missouri, the extension of the right to give the truth in evidence is more at large, and applies to all prosecutions or indictments for libels, without any qualifications annexed in restraint of the privilege; and an act of the legislature of New Jersey, in 1799, allowed the same unrestricted privilege. The legislature of Pennsylvania, in 1809, went far beyond their own constitution, and declared by statute, that no person should be indictable for a publication on the official conduct of men in public trust; and that in all actions or criminal prosecutions for a libel, the defendant might plead the truth in justification, or give it in evidence. The decision of the Court of Errors of this state, in *Thorn v. Blanchard*, carried the toleration of a libellous publication to as great an extent as the Pennsylvania law; for it appeared to be the doctrine of a majority of the court, that where a person petitioned the council of appointment to remove a public officer for corruption in office, public policy would not permit the officer libelled to have any redress by private action, whether the charge was true or false, or the motives of the petitioner innocent or malicious. The English law on the point seems to be founded in a juster policy. Petitions to the king, or to parliament, or to the secretary at war, for the redress of any grievance, are privileged communications, and not actionable libels, provided the privilege be not abused; but if it appear that the communication was made maliciously, and without probable cause, the pretence under which it is made aggravates the case, and an action lies. The constitution of this state, as amended in 1821, is a little varied in its language from those provisions which have been mentioned, and is not quite so latitudinary in its indulgence as some of them. It declares, that "in all prosecutions or indictments for libels, the truth may be given in evidence to the jury; and if it shall appear to the jury, that the matter charged as libellous, is true, and was published with good motives, and for justifiable ends, the party shall be acquitted." These provisions in favour of giving the truth in evidence, are to be found only in those constitutions which have been promulgated long since our revolution; and the current of opinion seems to have been setting strongly, not only in favour of erecting barriers against any previous restraints upon publications, (and which was all that the earlier sages of the revolution had in view,) but in favour of the policy that would diminish or destroy altogether every obstacle or responsibility in the way of the publication of the truth. The subject is not without its difficulties, and it has been found embarrassing to preserve equally, and in just harmony and proportion, the protection which is due to character, and the protection which ought to be afforded to liberty of speech, and of the press. These rights are frequently brought into dangerous collision, and the tendency of measures in this country has been to relax too far the vigilance with which the common law surrounded and guarded character, while we are animated with a generous anxiety to maintain freedom of discussion. The constitution of this state makes the facts in every possible case a necessary subject of open investigation; and however improper or unfit those facts may be for public information, and however painful or injurious to the individuals concerned, yet it would seem, that they may, in the first instance, be laid bare before the jury. The facts are to go to them, at all events; for the jury are to determine, *as it shall appear to them*, whether the motives of the libeller were good, and his end justifiable.

The act of Congress of the 14th of July, 1798, made it an indictable offence to libel the government, or Congress, or the President of the United States; and it made it lawful for the defendant, upon the trial, to give in evidence in his defence, the truth of the matter contained in the publication charged as a libel. This act was, by the terms of it, *declaratory*, and it was intended to convey the sense of Congress, that in prosecutions of that kind it was the common right of the defendant to give the truth in evidence. So, the case of *The People v. Croswell*, in this state, was followed by an act of the legislature on the 6th of April, 1805, enacting and *declaring*, that in every prosecution, for a libel, (and which included public and private prosecutions) it should be lawful for the defendant to give in evidence in his defence the truth of the matter charged; but such evidence was not to be a justification, unless, on the trial, it should be made satisfactorily to appear, that the matter charged as libellous was published with good motives, and for justifiable ends; and this was the whole extent of the doctrine which had been claimed in favour of the press in the case of *The People v. Croswell*.

The Truth in Private Actions

There appears to have been some contrariety of opinion in the English books on the point, whether a defendant in a private action upon a libel, could be permitted to justify the charge, by pleading the truth. But the prevailing, and the better opinion is, that the truth may, in all cases, be pleaded by way of justification, in a private action for damages, arising from written or printed defamation, as well as in an action for slanderous words. The ground of the private action, is the injury which the party has sustained, and his consequent right to damages as a recompense for that injury; but if the charge, in its substance and measure, be true in point of fact, the law considers the plaintiff as coming into court without any equitable title to relief. And yet it is easy to be perceived, that in the case of libels upon private character, greater strictness as to allowing the truth in evidence, by way of justification, ought to be observed, than in the case of public prosecutions; for the public have no interest in the detail of private vices and defects, when the individual charged is not a candidate for any public trust; and publications of that kind, are apt to be infected with malice, and to be very injurious to the peace and happiness of families. If the libel was made, in order to expose to the public eye personal defects, or misfortunes, or vices, the proof of the truth of the charge would rather aggravate than lessen the baseness and evil tendency of the publication; and there is much justice and sound policy in the opinion, that in private, as well as public prosecutions for libels, the inquiry should be pointed to the innocence or malice of the publisher's intentions. The truth ought to be admissible in evidence to explain that intent, and not in every instance to justify it. The guilt and the essential ground of action for defamation, consist in the malicious intention; and when the mind is not in fault, no prosecution can be sustained. On the other hand, the truth may be printed and published maliciously, and with an evil intent, and for no good purpose, and when it would be productive only of private misery, and public scandal and disgrace.

CHAPTER TWO

The Supreme Court and the Press in the Twentieth Century

The Bill of Rights

State Governments Cannot Exercise Prior Restraint

Charles Evans Hughes

Using the authority of a statute it had enacted, the state of Minnesota shut down a publication called the *Saturday Press* in 1927. The state charged that the publication had insinuated in its articles that local law enforcement was under the control of gangsters. The publishers appealed, and the case eventually reached the Supreme Court in 1931.

Chief Justice Charles Evans Hughes delivered the majority opinion in the case, excerpted below. The Court held that the state was not able to exercise such control over the press. It could resort to the laws of defamation, but could not stop the printing of the publication.

This case ruled definitively that not only the federal government was bound by the First Amendment; all states were also so bound by virtue of the Fourteenth Amendment. Therefore, even state legislatures were unable to exercise prior restraint against the press. This ruling was a victory for the press in general. However, by the time the lawsuit came to its completion at the Supreme Court level, the *Saturday Press* was bankrupt.

Hughes was an associate justice of the Supreme Court from 1910 to 1916 and chief justice from 1930 to 1941.

This statute, for the suppression as a public nuisance of a newspaper or periodical, is unusual, if not unique, and raises questions of grave importance transcending the local interests involved in the particular action. It is no longer open to doubt that the liberty of the press and of speech is within the liberty safeguarded by the due process clause of

Charles Evans Hughes, majority opinion, *Near v. State of Minnesota,* U.S. Supreme Court, Washington, DC, 1931.

the Fourteenth Amendment from invasion by state action. It was found impossible to conclude that this essential personal liberty of the citizen was left unprotected by the general guaranty of fundamental rights of person and property. In maintaining this guaranty, the authority of the state to enact laws to promote the health, safety, morals, and general welfare of its people is necessarily administered. The limits of this sovereign power must always be determined with appropriate regard to the particular subject of its exercise. Liberty of speech and of the press is . . . not an absolute right, and the state may punish its abuse. Liberty, in each of its phases, has its history and connotation, and, in the present instance, the inquiry is as to the historic conception of the liberty of the press and whether the statute under review violates the essential attributes of that liberty. . . .

The Statute's Operation and Effect

If we cut through mere details of procedure, the operation and effect of the statute in substance is that public authorities may bring the owner or publisher of a newspaper or periodical before a judge upon a charge of conducting a business of publishing scandalous and defamatory matter—in particular that the matter consists of charges against public officers of official dereliction—and, unless the owner or publisher is able and disposed to bring competent evidence to satisfy the judge that the charges are true and are published with good motives and for justifiable ends, his newspaper or periodical is suppressed and further publication is made punishable as a contempt. This is of the essence of censorship.

The question is whether a statute authorizing such proceedings in restraint of publication is consistent with the conception of the liberty of the press as historically conceived and guaranteed. In determining the extent of the constitutional protection, it has been generally, if not universally, considered that it is the chief purpose of the guaranty to prevent previous restraints upon publication. The struggle in England, directed against the legislative power of the licenser, resulted in renunciation of the censorship of the press. The liberty deemed to be established was thus described by [William]

Blackstone: 'The liberty of the press is indeed essential to the nature of a free state; but this consists in laying no previous restraints upon publications, and not in freedom from censure for criminal matter when published. Every freeman has an undoubted right to lay what sentiments he pleases before the public; to forbid this, is to destroy the freedom of the press; but if he publishes what is improper, mischievous or illegal, he must take the consequence of his own temerity.' The distinction was early pointed out between the extent of the freedom with respect to censorship under our constitutional system and that enjoyed in England. Here, as [James] Madison said, 'the great and essential rights of the people are secured against legislative as well as against executive ambition. They are secured, not by laws paramount to prerogative, but by constitutions paramount to laws. This security of the freedom of the press requires that it should be exempt not only from previous restraint by the Executive, as in Great Britain, but from legislative restraint also.' This Court said, in *Patterson v. Colorado*, 'In the first place, the main purpose of such constitutional provisions is "to prevent all such previous restraints upon publications as had been practiced by other governments," and they do not prevent the subsequent punishment of such as may be deemed contrary to the public welfare. The preliminary freedom extends as well to the false as to the true; the subsequent punishment may extend as well to the true as to the false. This was the law of criminal libel apart from statute in most cases, if not in all.'

The criticism upon Blackstone's statement has not been because immunity from previous restraint upon publication has not been regarded as deserving of special emphasis, but chiefly because that immunity cannot be deemed to exhaust the conception of the liberty guaranteed by State and Federal Constitutions. The point of criticism has been 'that the mere exemption from restraints cannot be all that is secured by the constitutional provisions,' and that 'the liberty of the press might be rendered a mockery and a delusion, and the phrase itself a by-word, if, while every man was at liberty to publish what he pleased, the public authorities might nevertheless punish him for harmless publications.' But it is recognized that punishment for the abuse of the liberty accorded to the press is essential to the protection of the public, and that the common-law rules that subject the libeler to responsibility for the public offense, as well as for the private injury, are not abolished by the protection extended in our Constitutions. The law of criminal libel rests upon that secure foundation. There is also the conceded authority of courts to punish for contempt when publications directly tend to prevent the proper discharge of judicial functions. In the present case, we have no occasion to inquire as to the permissible scope of subsequent punishment. For whatever wrong the appellant has committed or may commit, by his publications, the state appropriately affords both public and private redress by its libel laws. As has been noted, the statute in question does not deal with punishments; it provides for no punishment, except in case of contempt for violation of the court's order, but for suppression and injunction —that is, for restraint upon publication.

Prior Restraint Is Not Absolutely Prohibited

The objection has also been made that the principle as to immunity from previous restraint is stated too broadly, if every such restraint is deemed to be prohibited. That is undoubtedly true; the protection even as to previous restraint is not absolutely unlimited. But the limitation has been recognized only in exceptional cases. 'When a nation is at war many things that might be said in time of peace are such a hindrance to its effort that their utterance will not be endured so long as men fight and that no Court could regard them as protected by any constitutional right' [*Schenck v. United States*]. No one would question but that a government might prevent actual obstruction to its recruiting service or the publication of the sailing dates of transports or the number and location of troops. On similar grounds, the primary requirements of decency may be enforced against obscene publications. The security of the community life may be protected against incitements to acts of violence and the overthrow by force of orderly government. [The Supreme Court has ruled that] the constitutional guaranty of free speech does not 'protect a man from an injunction against uttering words that may have all the effects of force.' These limitations are not applicable here. Nor are we now concerned with questions as to the extent of authority to prevent publications in order to protect private rights according to the principles governing the exercise of the jurisdiction of courts of equity.

The exceptional nature of its limitations places in a strong light the general conception that liberty of the press, historically considered and taken up by the Federal Constitution, has meant, principally although not exclusively, immunity from previous restraints or censorship. The conception of the liberty of the press in this country had broadened with the exigencies of the colonial period and with the efforts to secure freedom from oppressive administration. That liberty was especially cherished for the immunity it afforded from previous restraint of the publication of censure of public officers and charges of official misconduct. As was said by Chief Justice Parker, in *Commonwealth v. Blanding*, with respect to the Constitution of Massachusetts: 'Besides, it is well understood and received as a commentary on this provision for the liberty of the press, that it was intended to prevent all such previous restraints upon publications as had been practiced by other governments, and in early times here, to stifle the efforts of patriots towards enlightening their fellow subjects upon their rights and the duties of rulers. The liberty of the press was to be unrestrained, but he who used it was to be responsible in case of its abuse.' In the letter sent by the Continental Congress (October 26, 1774) to the Inhabitants of Quebec, referring to the 'five grate rights' it was said: 'The last right we shall mention, regards the freedom of the press. The importance of this consists, besides the advancement of truth, science, morality, and arts in general, in its diffusion of liberal sentiments on the administration of Government, its ready communication of thoughts between subjects, and its consequential promotion of union among them, whereby oppressive officers are shamed or intimidated, into more honourable and just modes of conducting affairs.' Madison, who was the leading spirit in the preparation of the First Amendment of the Federal Constitution, thus described the practice and sentiment which led to the guaranties of liberty of the press in State Constitutions: 'In every State, probable, in the Union, the press has exerted a freedom in canvassing the merits and measures of public men of every description which has not been confined to the strict limits of the common law. On this footing the freedom of the press has stood; on this footing it yet stands. . . . Some degree of abuse is inseparable from the proper use of everything, and in no instance is this more true than in that of the press. It has accordingly been decided by the practice of the States, that it is better to leave a few of its noxious branches to their luxuriant growth, than, by pruning them away, to injure the vigour of those yielding the proper fruits. And can the wisdom of this policy be doubted by any who reflect that to the press alone, chequered as it is with abuses, the world is indebted for all the triumphs which have been gained by reason and humanity over error and oppression; who reflect that to the same beneficent source the United States owe much of the lights which conducted them to the ranks of a free and independent nation, and which have improved their political system into a shape so auspicious to their happiness? Had "Sedition Acts," forbidding every publication that might bring the constituted agents into contempt or disrepute, or that might excite the hatred of the people against the authors of unjust or pernicious measures, been uniformly enforced against the press, might not the United States have been languishing at this day under the infirmities of a sickly Confederation? Might they not, possibly, be miserable colonies, groaning under a foreign yoke?'

A Long-Understood Position

The fact that for approximately one hundred and fifty years there has been almost an entire absence of attempts to impose previous restraints upon publications relating to the malfeasance of public officers is significant of the deepseated conviction that such restraints would violate constitutional right. Public officers, whose character and conduct remain open to debate and free discussion in the press, find their remedies for false accusations in actions under libel laws providing for redress and punishment, and not in proceedings to restrain the publication of newspapers and periodicals. The general principle that the constitutional guaranty of the liberty of the press gives immunity from previous restraints has been approved in many decisions under the provisions of state constitutions.

The importance of this immunity has not lessened. While reckless assaults upon public men, and efforts to bring obloquy upon those who are endeavoring faithfully to discharge official duties, exert a baleful influence and deserve the severest condemnation in public opinion, it cannot be said that this abuse is greater, and it is believed to be less, than that which characterized the period in which our institutions took shape. Meanwhile, the administration of government has become more complex, the opportunities for malfeasance and corruption have multiplied, crime has grown to most serious proportions, and the danger of its protection by unfaithful officials and of the impairment of the fundamental security of life and property by criminal alliances and official neglect, emphasizes the primary need of a vigilant and courageous press, expecially in great cities. The fact that the liberty of the press may be abused by miscreant purveyors of scandal does not make any the less necessary the immunity of the press from previous restraint in dealing with offical misconduct. Subsequent punishment for such abuses as may exist is the appropriate remedy, consistent with constitutional privilege.

The Statute Cannot Be Defended

In attempted justification of the statute, it is said that it deals not with publication per se, but with the 'business' of publishing defamation. If, however, the publisher has a constitutional right to publish, without previous restraint, an edition of his newspaper charging official derelictions, it cannot be denied that he may publish subsequent editions for the same purpose. He does not lose his right by exercising it. If his right exists, it may be exercised in publishing nine editions, as in this case, as well as in one edition. If previous restraint is permissible, it may be imposed at once; indeed, the wrong may be as serious in one publication as in several. Characterizing the publication as a business, and the business as a nuisance, does not permit an invasion of the constitutional immunity against restraint. Similarly, it does not matter that the newspaper or periodical is found to be 'largely' or 'chiefly' devoted to the publication of such derelictions. If the publisher has a right, without previous restraint, to publish them, his right cannot be deemed to be dependent upon his publishing something else, more or less, with the matter to which objection is made.

Nor can it be said that the constitutional freedom from previous restraint is lost because charges are made of derelictions which constitute crimes. With the multiplying provisions of penal codes, and of municipal charters and ordinances carrying penal sanctions, the conduct of public officers is very largely within the purview of criminal statutes. The freedom of the press from previous restraint has never been regarded as limited to such animadversions as lay outside the range of penal enactments. Historically, there is no such limitation; it is inconsistent with the reason which underlies the privilege, as the privilege so limited would be of slight value for the purposes for which it came to be established.

The statute in question cannot be justified by reason of the fact that the publisher is permitted to show, before injunction issues, that the matter published is true and is published with good motives and for justifiable ends. If such a statute, authorizing suppression and injunction on such a basis, is constitutionally valid, it would be equally permissible for the Legislature to provide that at any time the publisher of any newspaper could be brought before a court, or even an administrative officer (as the constitutional protection may not be regarded as resting on mere procedural details), and required to produce proof of the truth of his publication, or of what he intended to publish and of his motives, or stand enjoined. If this can be done, the Legislature may provide machinery for determining in the complete exercise of its discretion what are justifiable ends and restrain publication accordingly. And it would be but a step to a complete system of censorship. The recognition of authority to impose previous restraint upon publication in order to protect the community against the circulation of charges of misconduct, and especially of official misconduct, necessarily would carry with it the admission of the authority of the censor against which the constitutional barrier was erected. The preliminary freedom, by virtue of the very reason for its existence, does not depend, as this court has said, on proof of truth.

Equally unavailing is the insistence that the statute is designed to prevent the circulation of scandal which tends to disturb the public peace and to provoke assaults and the commission of crime. Charges of reprehensible conduct, and in particular of official malfeasance, unquestionably create a public scandal, but the theory of the constitutional guaranty is that even a more serious public evil would be caused by authority to prevent publication. 'To prohibit the intent to excite those unfavorable sentiments against those who administer the Government, is equivalent to a prohibition of the actual excitement of them; and to prohibit the actual excitement of them is equivalent to a prohibition of discussions having that tendency and effect; which, again, is equivalent to a protection of those who administer the Government, if they should at any time deserve the contempt or hatred of the people, against being exposed to it by free animadversions on their characters and conduct,' [as stated by James Madison]. There is nothing new in the fact that charges of reprehensible conduct may create resentment and the disposition to resort to violent means of redress, but this well-understood tendency did not alter the determination to protect the press against censorship and restraint upon publication. As was said in *New Yorker Staats-Zeitung v. Nolan*: 'If the township may prevent the circulation of a newspaper for no reason other than that some of its inhabitants may violently disagree with it, and resent it as circulation by resorting to physical violence, there is no limit to what may be prohibited.' The danger of violent reactions becomes greater with effective organization of defiant groups resenting exposure, and, if this consideration warranted legislative interference with the initial freedom of publication, the constitutional protection would be reduced to a mere form of words.

For these reasons we hold the statute, so far as it author-ized the proceedings in this action . . . to be an infringement of the liberty of the press guaranteed by the Fourteenth Amendment. We should add that this decision rests upon the operation and effect of the statute, without regard to the ques-tion of the truth of the charges contained in the particular pe-riodical. The fact that the public officers named in this case, and those associated with the charges of official dereliction, may be deemed to be impeccable, cannot affect the conclusion that the statute imposes an unconstitutional restraint upon publication.

Freedom of the Press Does Not Extend to Obscenity

William J. Brennan

Most agree that the news media should have a wide scope to disseminate information. However, some argue that the publishing of obscenity or pornography should be limited or restrained in the interests of the public.

Samuel Roth published a magazine that contained literary erotica and nude pictures. He was charged under a federal statute for sending prohibited items through the mail. David Alberts, who also published a magazine that contained revealing pictures of women, was charged under a California obscenity law. Both appealed their convictions. The Supreme Court combined the cases because of their similar subject matter and ruled on them in *Roth v. United States* in 1957.

In the following excerpt from the case, Supreme Court justice William J. Brennan defines the scope of protected free speech and press and finds that obscenity is not a protected form of expression under the First Amendment.

[S]amuel] Roth conducted a business in New York in the publication and sale of books, photographs and magazines. He used circulars and advertising matter to solicit sales. He was convicted by a jury in the District Court for the Southern District of New York upon 4 counts of a 26-count indictment charging him with mailing obscene circulars and advertising, and an obscene book, in violation of the federal obscenity statute. His conviction was affirmed by the Court of Appeals for the Second Circuit. We granted certiorari [the right to review the trial record of the lower court's decision]. [David] Alberts conducted a mail-order business from Los An-

William J. Brennan, majority opinion, *Roth v. United States,* U.S. Supreme Court, Washington, DC, 1957.

geles. He was convicted by the Judge of the Municipal Court of the Beverly Hills Judicial District (having waived a jury trial) under a misdemeanor complaint which charged him with lewdly keeping for sale obscene and indecent books, and with writing, composing and publishing an obscene advertisement of them, in violation of the California Penal Code. The conviction was affirmed by the Appellate Department of the Superior Court of the State of California in and for the County of Los Angeles. We noted probable jurisdiction.

The dispositive question is whether obscenity is utterance within the area of protected speech and press. Although this is the first time the question has been squarely presented to this Court, either under the First Amendment or under the Fourteenth Amendment, expressions found in numerous opinions indicate that this Court has always assumed that obscenity is not protected by the freedoms of speech and press. . . .

The Protection of Press

The protection given speech and press was fashioned to assure unfettered interchange of ideas for the bringing about of political and social changes desired by the people. This objective was made explicit as early as 1774 in a letter of the Continental Congress to the inhabitants of Quebec:

> The last right we shall mention, regards the freedom of the press. The importance of this consists, besides the advancement of truth, science, morality, and arts in general, in its diffusion of liberal sentiments on the administration of Government, its ready communication of thoughts between subjects, and its consequential promotion of union among them, whereby oppressive officers are shamed or intimidated, into more honourable and just modes of conducting affairs.

All ideas having even the slightest redeeming social importance—unorthodox ideas, controversial ideas, even ideas hateful to the prevailing climate of opinion—have the full protection of the guaranties, unless excludable because they encroach upon the limited area of more important interests. But implicit in the history of the First Amendment is the rejection of obscenity as utterly without redeeming social importance. This rejection for that reason is mirrored in the universal judgment that obscenity should be restrained, reflected in the international agreement of over 50 nations, in the obscenity laws of all of the 48 States, and in the 20 obscenity laws enacted by the Congress from 1842 to 1956. This is the same judgment expressed by this Court in *Chaplinsky v. New Hampshire:*

> There are certain well-defined and narrowly limited classes of speech, the prevention and punishment of which have never been thought to raise any Constitutional problem. These include the lewd and obscene. . . . It has been well observed that such utterances are no essential part of any exposition of ideas, and are of such slight social value as a step to truth that any benefit that may be derived from them is clearly outweighed by the social interest in order and morality.

We hold that obscenity is not within the area of constitutionally protected speech or press.

No Need to Prove Clear and Present Danger

It is strenuously urged that these obscenity statutes offend the constitutional guaranties because they punish incitation to impure sexual thoughts, not shown to be related to any overt antisocial conduct which is or may be incited in the persons stimulated to such thoughts. In *Roth*, the trial judge instructed the jury: "The words 'obscene, lewd and lascivious' as used in the law, signify that form of immorality which has relation to sexual impurity and has a tendency to excite lustful thoughts." In *Alberts*, the trial judge applied the test laid down in *People v. Wepplo*, namely, whether the material has "a substantial tendency to deprave or corrupt its readers by inciting lascivious thoughts or arousing lustful desires." It is insisted that the constitutional guaranties are violated because convictions may be had without proof either that obscene material will perceptibly create a clear and present danger of antisocial conduct, or will probably induce its recipients to such conduct. But, in light of our holding that obscenity is not protected speech, the complete answer to this argument is in the holding of this Court in *Beauharnais v. Illinois*:

> Libelous utterances not being within the area of constitutionally protected speech, it is unnecessary, either for us or for the State courts, to consider the issues behind the phrase "clear and present danger." Certainly no one would contend that obscene speech, for example, may be punished only upon a showing of such circumstances. Libel, as we have seen, is in the same class.

What Is Obscenity?

However, sex and obscenity are not synonymous. Obscene material is material which deals with sex in a manner appealing to prurient interest. The portrayal of sex, e.g., in art, literature and scientific works, is not itself sufficient reason to deny material the constitutional protection of freedom of speech and press. Sex, a great and mysterious motive force in human life, has indisputably been a subject of absorbing interest to mankind through the ages; it is one of the vital problems of human interest and public concern. As to all such problems, this Court said in *Thornhill v. Alabama:*

> The freedom of speech and of the press guaranteed by the Constitution embraces at the least the liberty to discuss publicly and truthfully all matters of public concern without previous restraint or fear of subsequent punishment. The exigencies of the colonial period and the efforts to secure freedom from oppressive administration developed a broadened conception of these liberties as adequate to supply the public need for information and education with respect to the significant issues of the times. . . . Freedom of discussion, if it would fulfill its historic function in this nation, must embrace all issues about which information is needed or appropriate to enable the members of society to cope with the exigencies of their period.

The fundamental freedoms of speech and press have contributed greatly to the development and well-being of our free society and are indispensable to its continued growth. Ceaseless vigilance is the watchword to prevent their erosion by Congress or by the States. The door barring federal and state intrusion into this area cannot be left ajar; it must be kept tightly closed and opened only the slightest crack necessary to prevent encroachment upon more important interests. It is therefore vital that the standards for judging obscenity safeguard the protection of freedom of speech and press for material which does not treat sex in a manner appealing to prurient interest.

The early leading standard of obscenity [established in *Regina v. Hicklin*] allowed material to be judged merely by the effect of an isolated excerpt upon particularly susceptible persons. Some American courts adopted this standard but later decisions have rejected it and substituted this test: whether to the average person, applying contemporary community standards, the dominant theme of the material taken as a whole appeals to prurient interest. The *Hicklin* test, judging obscenity by the effect of isolated passages upon the most susceptible persons, might well encompass material legitimately treating with sex, and so it must be rejected as unconstitutionally restrictive of the freedoms of speech and press. On the other hand, the substituted standard provides safeguards adequate to withstand the charge of constitutional infirmity.

Both trial courts below sufficiently followed the proper standard. Both courts used the proper definition of obscenity. In addition, in the *Alberts* case, in ruling on a motion to dismiss, the trial judge indicated that, as the trier of facts, he was judging each item as a whole as it would affect the normal person, and in *Roth*, the trial judge instructed the jury as follows:

> The test is not whether it would arouse sexual desires or sexual impure thoughts in those comprising a particular segment of the community, the young, the immature or the highly prudish or would leave another segment, the scientific or highly educated or the so-called worldly-wise and sophisticated indifferent and unmoved. . . .

The test in each case is the effect of the book, picture or publication considered as a whole, not upon any particular class, but upon all those whom it is likely to reach. In other words, you determine its impact upon the average person in the community. The books, pictures and circulars must be judged as a whole, in their entire context, and you are not to consider detached or separate portions in reaching a conclusion. You judge the circulars, pictures and publications which have been put in evidence by present-day standards of the community. You may ask yourselves does it offend the common conscience of the community by present-day standards. . . .

In this case, ladies and gentlemen of the jury, you and you alone are the exclusive judges of what the common conscience of the community is, and in determining that conscience you are to consider the community as a whole, young and old, educated and uneducated, the religious and the irreligious—men, women and children.

Defining the Term "Obscenity"

It is argued that the statutes do not provide reasonably ascertainable standards of guilt and therefore violate the constitutional requirements of due process. The federal obscenity statute makes punishable the mailing of material that is "obscene, lewd, lascivious, or filthy . . . or other publication of an indecent character." The California statute makes punishable, inter alia [among other things], the keeping for sale or advertising material that is "obscene or indecent." The thrust of the argument is that these words are not sufficiently precise because they do not mean the same thing to all people, all the time, everywhere.

Many decisions have recognized that these terms of obscenity statutes are not precise. This Court, however, has consistently held that lack of precision is not itself offensive to the requirements of due process. ". . . The Constitution does not require impossible standards"; all that is required is that the language "conveys sufficiently definite warning as to the proscribed conduct when measured by common understanding and practices . . ." [*United States v. Petrillo*]. These words, applied according to the proper standard for judging obscenity, already discussed, give adequate warning of the conduct proscribed and mark ". . . boundaries sufficiently distinct for judges and juries fairly to administer the law. . . . That there may be marginal cases in which it is difficult to determine the side of the line on which a particular fact or situation falls is no sufficient reason to hold the language too ambiguous to define a criminal offense. . . ."

In summary, then, we hold that these statutes, applied according to the proper standard for judging obscenity, do not offend constitutional safeguards against convictions based upon protected material, or fail to give men in acting adequate notice of what is prohibited.

Roth's argument that the federal obscenity statute unconstitutionally encroaches upon the powers reserved by the Ninth and Tenth Amendments to the States and to the people to punish speech and press where offensive to decency and morality is hinged upon his contention that obscenity is expression not excepted from the sweep of the provision of the First Amendment that "Congress shall make no law . . . abridging the freedom of speech, or of the press. . . ." That argument falls in light of our holding that obscenity is not expression protected by the First Amendment. We therefore hold that the federal obscenity statute punishing the use of the mails for obscene material is a proper exercise of the postal power delegated to Congress. . . .

The judgments are Affirmed.

The Supreme Court Sets a New Standard for Libel

William J. Brennan

During the civil rights movement, the *New York Times* was paid to run an advertisement by a group that criticized the treatment of African American protesters in Montgomery, Alabama. The advertisement contained a number of allegations that were eventually found to be inaccurate. L.B. Sullivan, an elected commissioner of the city of Montgomery, Alabama, launched a lawsuit against the paper for libel and defamation, stating that the allegations in the advertisement were directed at him. Sullivan won the case, but the *New York Times* appealed, and the case eventually reached the Supreme Court.

In *New York Times v. Sullivan*, the Court ruled that the newspaper could not be sanctioned for libel even though it published factual errors that could have harmed a public official. In order to collect damages for libel, the claimant must prove that the press operated with "actual malice"—that is, knowingly publishing false statements. This ruling set a new standard that made libel much harder to prove. William J. Brennan served on the Court from 1956 to 1990.

Under Alabama law as applied in this case, a publication is "libelous per se" if the words "tend to injure a person . . . in his reputation" or to "bring [him] into public contempt"; the trial court stated that the standard was met if the words are such as to "injure him in his public office, or impute misconduct to him in his office, or want of official integrity, or want of fidelity to a public trust. . . ." The jury must find that the words were published "of and concerning" the plaintiff,

William J. Brennan, plurality opinion, *New York Times Co. v. Sullivan*, U.S. Supreme Court, Washington, DC, 1964.

but where the plaintiff is a public official his place in the governmental hierarchy sufficient evidence to support a finding that his reputation has been affected by statements that reflect upon the agency of which he is in charge. Once "libel per se" has been established, the defendant has no defense as to stated facts unless he can persuade the jury that they were true in all their particulars. His privilege of "fair comment" for expressions of opinion depends on the truth of the facts upon which the comment is based. *Parsons v. Age-Herald Publishing Co.* (1913). Unless he can discharge the burden of proving truth, general damages are presumed, and may be awarded without proof of pecuniary injury. A showing of actual malice is apparently a prerequisite to recovery of punitive damages, and the defendant may in any event forestall a punitive award by a retraction meeting the statutory requirements. Good motives and belief in truth do not negate an inference of malice, but are relevant only in mitigation of punitive damages if the jury chooses to accord them weight.

The question before us is whether this rule of liability, as applied to an action brought by a public official against critics of his official conduct, abridges the freedom of speech and of the press that is guaranteed by the First and Fourteenth Amendments.

Respondent [Sullivan] relies heavily, as did the Alabama courts, on statements of this Court to the effect that the Constitution does not protect libelous publications. Those statements do not foreclose our inquiry here. None of the cases sustained the use of libel laws to impose sanctions upon expression critical of the official conduct of public officials. The dictum in *Pennekamp v. Florida*, that "when the statements amount to defamation, a judge has such remedy in damages for libel as do other public servants," implied no view as to what remedy might constitutionally be afforded to public officials. In *Beauharnais v. Illinois*, the Court sustained an Illinois criminal libel statute as applied to a publication held to be both defamatory of a racial group and "liable to cause violence and disorder." But the Court was careful to note that it "retains and exercises authority to nullify action which encroaches on freedom of utterance under the guise of punishing libel"; for "public men, are, as it were, public property," and "discussion cannot be denied and the right, as well as the duty, of criticism must not be stifled." In the only previous case that did present the question of constitutional limitations upon the power to award damages for libel of a public official, the Court was equally divided and the question was not decided. In deciding the question now, we are compelled by neither precedent nor policy to give any more weight to the epithet "libel" than we have to other "mere labels" of state law. Like insurrection, contempt, advocacy of unlawful acts, breach of the peace, obscenity, solicitation of legal business, and the various other formulae for the repression of expression that have been challenged in this Court, libel can claim no talismanic immunity from constitutional limitations. It must be measured by standards that satisfy the First Amendment.

The First Amendment Guarantee

The general proposition that freedom of expression upon public questions is secured by the First Amendment has long been settled by our decisions. The constitutional safeguard, we have said, "was fashioned to assure unfettered interchange of ideas for the bringing about of political and social changes desired by the people." *Roth v. United States.* "The maintenance of the opportunity for free political discussion to the end that government may be responsive to the will of the people and that changes may be obtained by lawful means, an opportunity essential to the security of the Republic, is a fundamental principle of our constitutional system." *Stromberg v. California.* "It is a prized American privilege to speak one's mind, although not always with perfect good taste, on all public institutions," *Bridges v. California,* and this opportunity is to be afforded for "vigorous advocacy" no less than "abstract discussion." *N.A.A.C.P. v. Button.* The First Amendment, said Judge Learned Hand, "presupposes that right conclusions are more likely to be gathered out of a multitude of tongues, than through any kind of authoritative selection. To many this is, and always will be, folly; but we have staked upon it our all." *United States v. Associated Press.* Mr. Justice [Louis] Brandeis, in his concurring opinion in *Whitney v. California*, gave the principle its classic formulation:

> Those who won our independence believed . . . that public discussion is a political duty; and that this should be a fundamental principle of the American government. They recognized the risks to which all human institutions are subject. But they knew that order cannot be secured merely through fear of punishment for its infraction; that it is hazardous to discourage thought, hope and imagination; that fear breeds repression; that repression breeds hate; that hate menaces stable government; that the path of safety lies in the opportunity to discuss freely supposed grievances and proposed remedies; and that the fitting remedy for evil counsels is good ones. Believing in the power of reason as applied through public discussion, they eschewed silence coerced by law—the argument of force in its worst form. Recognizing the occasional tyrannies of governing majorities, they amended the Constitution so that free speech and assembly should be guaranteed.

Thus we consider this case against the background of a profound national commitment to the principle that debate on public issues should be uninhibited, robust, and wide-open, and that it may well include vehement, caustic, and sometimes unpleasantly sharp attacks on government and public officials. The present advertisement, as an expression of grievance and protest on one of the major public issues of our time, would seem clearly to qualify for the constitutional protection. The question is whether it forfeits that protection by the falsity of some of its factual statements and by its alleged defamation of respondent.

Erroneous Statement Is Inevitable

Authoritative interpretations of the First Amendment guarantees have consistently refused to recognize an exception for any test of truth—whether administered by judges, juries, or administrative officials—and especially one that puts the burden of proving truth on the speaker. The constitutional protection does not turn upon "the truth, popularity, or social utility of the ideas and beliefs which are offered." *N.A.A.C.P. v. Button*. As [James] Madison said, "Some degree of abuse is inseparable from the proper use of every thing; and in no instance is this more true than in that of the press." In *Cantwell v. Connecticut*, the Court declared:

> In the realm of religious faith, and in that of political belief, sharp differences arise. In both fields the tenets of one man may seem the rankest error to his neighbor. To persuade others to his own point of view, the pleader, as we know, at times, resorts to exaggeration, to vilification of men who have been, or are, prominent in church or state, and even to false statement. But the people of this nation have ordained in the light of history, that, in spite of the probability of excesses and abuses, these liberties are, in the long view, essential to enlightened opinion and right conduct on the part of the citizens of a democracy.

That erroneous statement is inevitable in free debate, and that it must be protected if the freedoms of expression are to have the "breathing space" that they "need . . . to survive" [*N.A.A.C.P. v. Button*], was also recognized by the Court of Appeals for the District of Columbia Circuit in *Sweeney v. Patterson*. Judge Edgerton spoke for a unanimous court which affirmed the dismissal of a Congressman's libel suit based upon a newspaper article charging him with anti-Semitism in opposing a judicial appointment. He said:

> Cases which impose liability for erroneous reports of the political conduct of officials reflect the obsolete doctrine that the governed must not criticize their governors. . . . The interest of the public here outweighs the interest of appellant or any other individual. The protection of the public requires not merely discussion, but information. Political conduct and views which some respectable people approve, and others condemn, are constantly imputed to Congressmen. Errors of fact, particularly in regard to a man's mental states and

> processes, are inevitable. . . . Whatever is added to the
> field of libel is taken from the field of free debate.

Injury to official reputation affords no more warrant for re-
pressing speech that would otherwise be free than does factual error. Where judicial officers are involved, this Court
has held that concern for the dignity and reputation of the
courts does not justify the punishment as criminal contempt
of criticism of the judge or his decision. *Bridges v. California.*
This is true even though the utterance contains "half-truths"
and "misinformation." *Pennekamp v. Florida.* Such repression can be justified, if at all, only by a clear and present danger of the obstruction of justice. If judges are to be treated as
"men of fortitude, able to thrive in a hardy climate," *Craig v.
Harney*, surely the same must be true of other government
officials, such as elected city commissioners. Criticism of
their official conduct does not lose its constitutional protection merely because it is effective criticism and hence dimin-
ishes their official reputations.

A Fundamental Principle

If neither factual error nor defamatory content suffices to remove the constitutional shield from criticism of official conduct,
the combination of the two elements is no less inadequate.
This is the lesson to be drawn from the great controversy over
the Sedition Act of 1798, which first crystallized a national
awareness of the central meaning of the First Amendment.
That statute made it a crime, punishable by a $5,000 fine
and five years in prison, "if any person shall write, print,
utter or publish . . . any false, scandalous and malicious writing or writings against the government of the United States,
or either house of the Congress . . . , or the President . . . ,
with intent to defame . . . or to bring them, or either of them,
into contempt or disrepute; or to excite against them, or either or any of them, the hatred of the good people of the
United States." The Act allowed the defendant the defense of
truth, and provided that the jury were to be judges both of
the law and the facts. Despite these qualifications, the Act
was vigorously condemned as unconstitutional in an attack

joined in by [Thomas] Jefferson and Madison. In the famous Virginia Resolutions of 1798, the General Assembly of Virginia resolved that it

> doth particularly protest against the palpable and alarming infractions of the Constitution, in the two late cases of the "Alien and Sedition Acts," passed at the last session of Congress. . . . [The Sedition Act] exercises . . . a power not delegated by the Constitution, but, on the contrary, expressly and positively forbidden by one of the amendments thereto—a power which, more than any other, ought to produce universal alarm, because it is levelled against the right of freely examining public characters and measures, and of free communication among the people thereon, which has ever been justly deemed the only effectual guardian of every other right.

Madison prepared the Report in support of the protest. His premise was that the Constitution created a form of government under which "The people, not the government, possess the absolute sovereignty." The structure of the government dispersed power in reflection of the people's distrust of concentrated power, and of power itself at all levels. This form of government was "altogether different" from the British form, under which the Crown was sovereign and the people were subjects. "Is it not natural and necessary, under such different circumstances," he asked, "that a different degree of freedom in the use of the press should be contemplated?" Earlier, in a debate in the House of Representatives, Madison had said: "If we advert to the nature of Republican Government, we shall find that the censorial power is in the people over the Government, and not in the Government over the people." Of the exercise of that power by the press, his Report said: "In every state, probably, in the Union, the press has exerted a freedom in canvassing the merits and measures of public men, of every description, which has not been confined to the strict limits of the common law. On this footing the freedom of the press has stood; on this foundation it yet stands. . . ." The right of free public discussion of the stewardship of public officials was thus, in Madison's view, a fundamental principle of the American form of government. . . .

There is no force in respondent's argument that the constitutional limitations implicit in the history of the Sedition Act apply only to Congress and not to the States. It is true that the First Amendment was originally addressed only to action by the Federal Government, and that Jefferson, for one, while denying the power of Congress "to controul the freedom of the press," recognized such a power in the States. But this distinction was eliminated with the adoption of the Fourteenth Amendment and the application to the States of the First Amendment's restrictions.

Encouraging Self-Censorship

What a State may not constitutionally bring about by means of a criminal statute is likewise beyond the reach of its civil law of libel. The fear of damage awards under a rule such as that invoked by the Alabama courts here may be markedly more inhibiting than the fear of prosecution under a criminal statute. Alabama, for example, has a criminal libel law which subjects to prosecution "any person who speaks, writes, or prints of and concerning another any accusation falsely and maliciously importing the commission by such person of a felony, or any other indictable offense involving moral turpitude," and which allows as punishment upon conviction a fine not exceeding $500 and a prison sentence of six months. Presumably a person charged with violation of this statute enjoys ordinary criminal-law safeguards such as the requirements of an indictment and of proof beyond a reasonable doubt. These safeguards are not available to the defendant in a civil action. The judgment awarded in this case —without the need for any proof of actual pecuniary loss— was one thousand times greater than the maximum fine provided by the Alabama criminal statute, and one hundred times greater than that provided by the Sedition Act. And since there is no double-jeopardy limitation applicable to civil lawsuits, this is not the only judgment that may be awarded against petitioners for the same publication. Whether or not a newspaper can survive a succession of such judgments, the pall of fear and timidity imposed upon those who would give voice to public criticism is an atmosphere in which the First Amendment freedoms cannot survive. Plainly the Alabama law of civil libel is "a form of regulation that creates hazards to protected freedoms markedly greater than those that attend reliance upon the criminal law." *Bantam Books, Inc. v. Sullivan.*

The state rule of law is not saved by its allowance of the defense of truth. A defense for erroneous statements honestly made is no less essential here than was the requirement of proof of guilty knowledge which, in *Smith v. California*, we held indispensable to a valid conviction of a bookseller for possessing obscene writings for sale. We said:

> For if the bookseller is criminally liable without knowledge of the contents, . . . he will tend to restrict the books he sells to those he has inspected; and thus the State will have imposed a restriction upon the distribution of constitutionally protected as well as obscene literature. . . . And the bookseller's burden would become the public's burden, for by restricting him the public's access to reading matter would be restricted. . . . His timidity in the face of his absolute criminal liability, thus would tend to restrict the public's access to forms of the printed word which the State could not constitutionally suppress directly. The bookseller's self-censorship, compelled by the State, would be a censorship affecting the whole public, hardly less virulent for being privately administered. Through it, the distribution of all books, both obscene and not obscene, would be impeded.

A rule compelling the critic of official conduct to guarantee the truth of all his factual assertions—and to do so on pain of libel judgments virtually unlimited in amount—leads to a comparable "self-censorship." Allowance of the defense of truth, with the burden of proving it on the defendant, does not mean that only false speech will be deterred. Even courts accepting this defense as an adequate safeguard have recognized the difficulties of adducing legal proofs that the alleged libel was true in all its factual particulars. Under such a rule, would-be critics of official conduct may be deterred from voicing their criticism, even though it is believed to be true and even though it is in fact true, because of doubt whether it can be proved in court or fear of the expense of having to do so. They tend to make only statements which "steer far wider of the unlawful zone." *Speiser v. Randall.* The rule thus dampens the vigor and limits the variety of public debate. It is inconsistent with the First and Fourteenth Amendments.

Proof of Actual Malice Is Required

The constitutional guarantees require, we think, a federal rule that prohibits a public official from recovering damages for a defamatory falsehood relating to his official conduct unless he proves that the statement was made with "actual malice"—that is, with knowledge that it was false or with reckless disregard of whether it was false or not. An oft-cited statement of a like rule, which has been adopted by a number of state courts, is found in the Kansas case of *Coleman v. MacLennan.* The State Attorney General, a candidate for reelection and a member of the commission charged with the management and control of the state school fund, sued a newspaper publisher for alleged libel in an article purporting to state facts relating to his official conduct in connection with a school-fund transaction. The defendant pleaded privilege and the trial judge, over the plaintiff's objection, instructed the jury that

> where an article is published and circulated among voters for the sole purpose of giving what the defendant believes to be truthful information concerning a candidate for public office and for the purpose of enabling such voters to cast their ballot more intelligently, and the whole thing is done in good faith and without malice, the article is privileged, although the principal matters contained in the article may be untrue in fact and derogatory to the character of the plaintiff; and in such a case the burden is on the plaintiff to show actual malice in the publication of the article.

In answer to a special question, the jury found that the plaintiff had not proved actual malice, and a general verdict was returned for the defendant. On appeal the Supreme Court of Kansas, in an opinion by Justice Burch, reasoned as follows:

> It is of the utmost consequence that the people should discuss the character and qualifications of candidates for their suffrages. The importance to the state and to society of such discussions is so vast, and the advantages derived are so great, that they more than counterbalance the inconvenience of private persons whose conduct may be involved, and occasional injury to the reputations of individuals must yield to the public welfare, although at times such injury may be great. The public benefit from publicity is so great, and the chance of injury to private character so small, that such discussion must be privileged.

The court thus sustained the trial court's instruction as a correct statement of the law, saying: "In such a case the occasion gives rise to a privilege, qualified to this extent: any one claiming to be defamed by the communication must show actual malice or go remediless. This privilege extends to a great variety of subjects, and includes matters of public concern, public men, and candidates for office."

Such a privilege for criticism of official conduct is appropriately analogous to the protection accorded a public official when he is sued for libel by a private citizen. In *Barr v. Matteo*, this Court held the utterance of a federal official to be absolutely privileged if made "within the outer perimeter" of his duties. The States accord the same immunity to statements of their highest officers, although some differentiate their lesser officials and qualify the privilege they enjoy. But all hold that all officials are protected unless actual malice can be proved. The reason for the official privilege is said to be that the threat of damage suits would otherwise "inhibit the fearless, vigorous, and effective administration of policies of government" and "dampen the ardor of all but the most resolute, or the most irresponsible, in the unflinching discharge of their duties." *Barr v. Matteo*. Analogous considerations support the privilege for the citizen-critic of government. It is as much his duty to criticize as it is the official's duty to administer. As Madison said, "the censorial power is in the people over the Government, and not in the Government over the people." It would give public servants an unjustified preference over the public they serve, if critics of official conduct did not have a fair equivalent of the immunity granted to the officials themselves.

We conclude that such a privilege is required by the First and Fourteenth Amendments.

Balancing Freedom of the Press and the Rights of the Accused

Tom C. Clarke

Sam Sheppard, a Cleveland doctor, was accused of killing his wife in 1954 and was subsequently tried. The trial judge, feeling bound by the First Amendment, gave free reign to the press, even giving them a special table in the courtroom. The press and other forms of media covered every possible aspect of the case, even publishing the names and addresses of potential jurors. After being convicted, Sheppard appealed to the Supreme Court on the grounds that he had not received a fair trial due to excessive prejudicial publicity. The Court ruled in his favor.

Tom C. Clarke delivered the judgment of the Supreme Court, concluding that the freedom of the press is not an absolute guarantee but must be balanced against the right of an accused person to a fair trial. In Clarke's opinion, the trial judge should have placed greater restraint over the actions of the press during the trial, if not the actual messages the press eventually delivered. This case set a precedent for restricted media coverage of trials. Sheppard was eventually retried and acquitted.

The courtroom in which the trial was held measured 26 by 48 feet. A long temporary table was set up inside the bar, in back of the single counsel table. It ran the width of the courtroom, parallel to the bar railing, with one end less than three feet from the jury box. Approximately 20 representatives of newspapers and wire services were assigned seats at this table

Tom C. Clarke, majority opinion, *Sheppard v. Maxwell*, U.S. Supreme Court, Washington, DC, 1966.

by the court. Behind the bar railing there were four rows of benches. These seats were likewise assigned by the court for the entire trial. The first row was occupied by representatives of television and radio stations, and the second and third rows by reporters from out-of-town newspapers and magazines. One side of the last row, which accommodated 14 people, was assigned to Sheppard's family and the other to [Sheppard's wife] Marilyn's. The public was permitted to fill vacancies in this row on special passes only. Representatives of the news media also used all the rooms on the courtroom floor, including the room where cases were ordinarily called and assigned for trial. Private telephone lines and telegraphic equipment were installed in these rooms so that reports from the trial could be speeded to the papers. Station WSRS was permitted to set up broadcasting facilities on the third floor of the courthouse next door to the jury room, where the jury rested during recesses in the trial and deliberated. Newscasts were made from this room throughout the trial, and while the jury reached its verdict.

On the sidewalk and steps in front of the courthouse, television and newsreel cameras were occasionally used to take motion pictures of the participants in the trial, including the jury and the judge. Indeed, one television broadcast carried a staged interview of the judge as he entered the courthouse. In the corridors outside the courtroom there was a host of photographers and television personnel with flash cameras, portable lights and motion picture cameras. This group photographed the prospective jurors during selection of the jury. After the trial opened, the witnesses, counsel, and jurors were photographed and televised whenever they entered or left the courtroom. Sheppard was brought to the courtroom about 10 minutes before each session began; he was surrounded by reporters and extensively photographed for the newspapers and television. A rule of court prohibited picture-taking in the courtroom during the actual sessions of the court, but no restraints were put on photographers during recesses, which were taken once each morning and afternoon, with a longer period for lunch.

All of these arrangements with the news media and their massive coverage of the trial continued during the entire nine weeks of the trial. The courtroom remained crowded to capacity with representatives of news media. Their movement in and out of the courtroom often caused so much confusion that, despite the loud-speaker system installed in the courtroom, it was difficult for the witnesses and counsel to be heard. Furthermore, the reporters clustered within the bar of the small courtroom made confidential talk among Sheppard and his counsel almost impossible during the proceedings. They frequently had to leave the courtroom to obtain privacy. And many times when counsel wished to raise a point with the judge out of the hearing of the jury it was necessary to move to the judge's chambers. Even then, news media representatives so packed the judge's anteroom that counsel could hardly return from the chambers to the courtroom. The reporters vied with each other to find out what counsel and the judge had discussed, and often these matters later appeared in newspapers accessible to the jury.

The daily record of the proceedings was made available to the newspapers and the testimony of each witness was printed verbatim in the local editions, along with objections of counsel, and rulings by the judge. Pictures of Sheppard, the judge, counsel, pertinent witnesses, and the jury often accompanied the daily newspaper and television accounts. At times the newspapers published photographs of exhibits introduced at the trial, and the rooms of Sheppard's house were featured along with relevant testimony.

The jurors themselves were constantly exposed to the news media. Every juror, except one, testified at voir dire to reading about the case in the Cleveland papers or to having heard broadcasts about it. Seven of the 12 jurors who rendered the verdict had one or more Cleveland papers delivered in their home; the remaining jurors were not interrogated on the point. Nor were there questions as to radios or television sets in the jurors' homes, but we must assume that most of them owned such conveniences. As the selection of the jury progressed, individual pictures of prospective members appeared daily. During the trial, pictures of the jury appeared over 40 times in the Cleveland papers alone. The court permitted photographers to take pictures of the jury in the box, and individual pictures of the members in the jury room. One newspaper ran pictures of the jurors at the Sheppard home when they went there to view the scene of the murder. Another paper featured the home life of an alternate juror. The day before the verdict was rendered—while the jurors were at lunch and sequestered by two bailiffs—the jury was separated into two groups to pose for photographs which appeared in the newspapers. . . .

The Application of Justice

The principle that justice cannot survive behind walls of silence has long been reflected in the "Anglo-American distrust for secret trials." *In re Oliver* (1948). A responsible press has always been regarded as the handmaiden of effective judicial administration, especially in the criminal field. Its function in this regard is documented by an impressive record of service over several centuries. The press does not simply publish information about trials but guards against the miscarriage of justice by subjecting the police, prosecutors, and judicial processes to extensive public scrutiny and criticism. This Court has, therefore, been unwilling to place any direct limitations on the freedom traditionally exercised by the news media for "what transpires in the court room is public property." *Craig v. Harney* (1947). The "unqualified prohibitions laid down by the framers were intended to give to liberty of the press . . . the broadest scope that could be countenanced in an orderly society." *Bridges v. California* (1941). And where there was "no threat or menace to the integrity of the trial," *Craig v. Harney*, we have consistently required that the press have a free hand, even though we sometimes deplored its sensationalism.

But the Court has also pointed out that "legal trials are not like elections, to be won through the use of the meeting-hall, the radio, and the newspaper." *Bridges v. California*. And the Court has insisted that no one be punished for a crime without "a charge fairly made and fairly tried in a public tribunal free of prejudice, passion, excitement, and tyrannical power." *Chambers v. Florida* (1940). "Freedom of discussion should be given the widest range compatible with the essential requirement of the fair and orderly administration of justice." *Pennekamp v. Florida* (1946). But it must not be allowed to divert the trial from the "very purpose of a court system . . . to adjudicate controversies, both criminal and civil, in the calmness and solemnity of the courtroom according to legal procedures." *Cox v. Louisiana* (1965). Among these "legal procedures" is the requirement that the jury's verdict be based on evidence received in open court, not from outside sources. Thus, in *Marshall v. United States* (1959), we set aside a federal conviction where the jurors were exposed "through news accounts" to information that was not admitted at trial. We held that the prejudice from such material "may indeed be greater" than when it is part of the prosecution's evidence "for it is then not tempered by protective procedures." At the same time, we did not consider dispositive the statement of each juror "that he would not be influenced by the news articles, that he could decide the case only on the evidence of record, and that he felt no prejudice against petitioner as a result of the articles." Likewise, in *Irvin v. Dowd* (1961), even though each juror indicated that he could render an impartial verdict despite exposure to prejudicial newspaper articles, we set aside the conviction holding: "With his life at stake, it is not requiring too much that petitioner be tried in an atmosphere undisturbed by so huge a wave of public passion."

The undeviating rule of this Court was expressed by Mr. Justice Holmes over half a century ago in *Patterson v. Colorado* (1907): "The theory of our system is that the conclusions to be reached in a case will be induced only by evidence and argument in open court, and not by any outside influence, whether of private talk or public print." . . .

The Actions of the Trial Judge
It is clear that the totality of circumstances in this case also warrants such an approach. . . . Sheppard was not granted a change of venue to a locale away from where the publicity originated; nor was his jury sequestered. . . . The Sheppard jurors were subjected to newspaper, radio and television coverage of the trial while not taking part in the proceedings.

They were allowed to go their separate ways outside of the courtroom, without adequate directions not to read or listen to anything concerning the case. The judge's "admonitions" at the beginning of the trial are representative:

> I would suggest to you and caution you that you do not read any newspapers during the progress of this trial, that you do not listen to radio comments nor watch or listen to television comments, insofar as this case is concerned. You will feel very much better as the trial proceeds. . . . I am sure that we shall all feel very much better if we do not indulge in any newspaper reading or listening to any comments whatever about the matter while the case is in progress. After it is all over, you can read it all to your heart's content.

At intervals during the trial, the judge simply repeated his "suggestions" and "requests" that the jurors not expose themselves to comment upon the case. Moreover, the jurors were thrust into the role of celebrities by the judge's failure to insulate them from reporters and photographers. See *Estes v. Texas*. The numerous pictures of the jurors, with their addresses, which appeared in the newspapers before and during the trial itself exposed them to expressions of opinion from both cranks and friends. The fact that anonymous letters had been received by prospective jurors should have made the judge aware that this publicity seriously threatened the jurors' privacy.

The press coverage of the *Estes* trial was not nearly as massive and pervasive as the attention given by the Cleveland newspapers and broadcasting stations to Sheppard's prosecution. Sheppard stood indicted for the murder of his wife; the State was demanding the death penalty. For months the virulent publicity about Sheppard and the murder had made the case notorious. Charges and countercharges were aired in the news media besides those for which Sheppard was called to trial. In addition, only three months before trial, Sheppard was examined for more than five hours without counsel during a three-day inquest which ended in a public brawl. The inquest was televised live from a high school gymnasium seating hundreds of people. Furthermore, the trial began two weeks before a hotly contested election at which both Chief Prosecutor Mahon and Judge Blythin were candidates for judgeships.

Bedlam Reigned at the Courthouse

While we cannot say that Sheppard was denied due process by the judge's refusal to take precautions against the influence of pretrial publicity alone, the court's later rulings must be considered against the setting in which the trial was held. In light of this background, we believe that the arrangements made by the judge with the news media caused Sheppard to be deprived of that "judicial serenity and calm to which [he] was entitled." *Estes v. Texas.* The fact is that bedlam reigned at the courthouse during the trial and newsmen took over practically the entire courtroom, hounding most of the participants in the trial, especially Sheppard. At a temporary table within a few feet of the jury box and counsel table sat some 20 reporters staring at Sheppard and taking notes. The erection of a press table for reporters inside the bar is unprecedented. The bar of the court is reserved for counsel, providing them a safe place in which to keep papers and exhibits, and to confer privately with client and co-counsel. It is designed to protect the witness and the jury from any distractions, intrusions or influences, and to permit bench discussions of the judge's rulings away from the hearing of the public and the jury. Having assigned almost all of the available seats in the courtroom to the news media the judge lost his ability to supervise that environment. The movement of the reporters in and out of the courtroom caused frequent confusion and disruption of the trial. And the record reveals constant commotion within the bar. Moreover, the judge gave the throng of newsmen gathered in the corridors of the courthouse absolute free rein. Participants in the trial, including the jury, were forced to run a gantlet of reporters and photographers each time they entered or left the courtroom. The total lack of consideration for the privacy of the jury was demonstrated by the assignment to a broadcasting station of space next to the jury room on the floor above the courtroom, as well as the fact that jurors were allowed to make telephone calls during their five-day deliberation.

The Nature of the Publicity

There can be no question about the nature of the publicity which surrounded Sheppard's trial. We agree, as did the Court of Appeals, with the findings in Judge Bell's opinion for the Ohio Supreme Court:

> Murder and mystery, society, sex and suspense were combined in this case in such a manner as to intrigue and captivate the public fancy to a degree perhaps unparalleled in recent annals. Throughout the preindictment investigation, the subsequent legal skirmishes and the nine-week trial, circulation-conscious editors catered to the insatiable interest of the American public in the bizarre. . . . In this atmosphere of a "Roman holiday" for the news media, Sam Sheppard stood trial for his life.

Indeed, every court that has considered this case, save the court that tried it, has deplored the manner in which the news media inflamed and prejudiced the public.

Much of the material printed or broadcast during the trial was never heard from the witness stand, such as the charges that Sheppard had purposely impeded the murder investigation and must be guilty since he had hired a prominent criminal lawyer; that Sheppard was a perjurer; that he had sexual relations with numerous women; that his slain wife had characterized him as a "Jekyll-Hyde"; that he was "a bare-faced liar" because of his testimony as to police treatment; and, finally, that a woman convict claimed Sheppard to be the father of her illegitimate child. As the trial progressed, the newspapers summarized and interpreted the evidence, devoting particular attention to the material that incriminated Sheppard, and often drew unwarranted inferences from testimony. At one point, a front-page picture of Mrs. Sheppard's blood-stained pillow was published after being "doctored" to show more clearly an alleged imprint of a surgical instrument.

Nor is there doubt that this deluge of publicity reached at least some of the jury. On the only occasion that the jury was queried, two jurors admitted in open court to hearing the highly inflammatory charge that a prison inmate claimed Sheppard as the father of her illegitimate child. Despite the extent and nature of the publicity to which the jury was exposed during trial, the judge refused defense counsel's other requests that the jurors be asked whether they had read or heard specific prejudicial comment about the case, including the incidents we have previously summarized. In these circumstances, we can assume that some of this material reached members of the jury.

The Trial Judge's Mistake

The court's fundamental error is compounded by the holding that it lacked power to control the publicity about the trial. From the very inception of the proceedings the judge announced that neither he nor anyone else could restrict prejudicial news accounts. And he reiterated this view on numerous occasions. Since he viewed the news media as his target, the judge never considered other means that are often utilized to reduce the appearance of prejudicial material and to protect the jury from outside influence. We conclude that these procedures would have been sufficient to guarantee Sheppard a fair trial and so do not consider what sanctions might be available against a recalcitrant press nor the charges of bias now made against the state trial judge.

The carnival atmosphere at trial could easily have been avoided since the courtroom and courthouse premises are subject to the control of the court. As we stressed in *Estes*, the presence of the press at judicial proceedings must be limited when it is apparent that the accused might otherwise be prejudiced or disadvantaged. Bearing in mind the massive pretrial publicity, the judge should have adopted stricter rules governing the use of the courtroom by newsmen, as Sheppard's counsel requested. The number of reporters in the courtroom itself could have been limited at the first sign that their presence would disrupt the trial. They certainly should not have been placed inside the bar. Furthermore, the judge should have more closely regulated the conduct of newsmen in the courtroom. For instance, the judge belatedly asked them not to handle and photograph trial exhibits lying on the counsel table during recesses.

Secondly, the court should have insulated the witnesses. All of the newspapers and radio stations apparently interviewed prospective witnesses at will, and in many instances disclosed their testimony. A typical example was the publication of numerous statements by Susan Hayes, before her appearance in court, regarding her love affair with Sheppard. Although the witnesses were barred from the courtroom during the trial the full verbatim testimony was available to them in the press. This completely nullified the judge's imposition of the rule.

Thirdly, the court should have made some effort to control the release of leads, information, and gossip to the press by police officers, witnesses, and the counsel for both sides. Much of the information thus disclosed was inaccurate, leading to groundless rumors and confusion. That the judge was aware of his responsibility in this respect may be seen from his warning to Steve Sheppard, the accused's brother, who had apparently made public statements in an attempt to discredit testimony for the prosecution. The judge made this statement in the presence of the jury:

Now, the Court wants to say a word. That he was told— he has not read anything about it at all—but he was informed that Dr. Steve Sheppard, who has been granted the privilege of remaining in the court room during the trial, has been trying the case in the newspapers and making rather uncomplimentary comments about the testimony of the witnesses for the State.

Let it be now understood that if Dr. Steve Sheppard wishes to use the newspapers to try his case while we are trying it here, he will be barred from remaining in the court room during the progress of the trial if he is to be a witness in the case.

The Court appreciates he cannot deny Steve Sheppard the right of free speech, but he can deny him the

... privilege of being in the court room, if he wants to avail himself of that method during the progress of the trial.

The Defense Position

Defense counsel immediately brought to the court's attention the tremendous amount of publicity in the Cleveland press that "misrepresented entirely the testimony" in the case. Under such circumstances, the judge should have at least warned the newspapers to check the accuracy of their accounts. And it is obvious that the judge should have further sought to alleviate this problem by imposing control over the statements made to the news media by counsel, witnesses, and especially the Coroner and police officers. The prosecution repeatedly made evidence available to the news media which was never offered in the trial. Much of the "evidence" disseminated in this fashion was clearly inadmissible. The exclusion of such evidence in court is rendered meaningless when news media make it available to the public. For example, the publicity about Sheppard's refusal to take a lie detector test came directly from police officers and the Coroner. The story that Sheppard had been called a "Jekyll-Hyde" personality by his wife was attributed to a prosecution witness. No such testimony was given. The further report that there was "a 'bombshell witness' on tap" who would testify as to Sheppard's "fiery temper" could only have emanated from the prosecution. Moreover, the newspapers described in detail clues that had been found by the police, but not put into the record.

The fact that many of the prejudicial news items can be traced to the prosecution, as well as the defense, aggravates the judge's failure to take any action. Effective control of these sources—concededly within the court's power—might well have prevented the divulgence of inaccurate information, rumors, and accusations that made up much of the inflammatory publicity, at least after Sheppard's indictment.

More specifically, the trial court might well have proscribed [prohibited] extrajudicial statements by any lawyer, party, witness, or court official which divulged prejudicial matters, such as the refusal of Sheppard to submit to interrogation or take any lie detector tests; any statement made by Sheppard to officials; the identity of prospective witnesses or their probable testimony; any belief in guilt or innocence; or like statements concerning the merits of the case. Being advised of the great public interest in the case, the mass coverage of the press, and the potential prejudicial impact of publicity, the court could also have requested the appropriate city and county officials to promulgate a regulation with respect to dissemination of information about the case by their employees. In addition, reporters who wrote or broadcast prejudicial stories, could have been warned as to the impropriety of publishing material not introduced in the proceedings. The judge was put on notice of such events by defense counsel's complaint about the WHK broadcast on the second day of trial. In this manner, Sheppard's right to a trial free from outside interference would have been given added protection without corresponding curtailment of the news media. Had the judge, the other officers of the court, and the police placed the interest of justice first, the news media would have soon learned to be content with the task of reporting the case as it unfolded in the courtroom—not pieced together from extrajudicial statements.

Looking Toward the Future

From the cases coming here we note that unfair and prejudicial news comment on pending trials has become increasingly prevalent. Due process requires that the accused receive a trial by an impartial jury free from outside influences. Given the pervasiveness of modern communications and the difficulty of effacing prejudicial publicity from the minds of the jurors, the trial courts must take strong measures to ensure that the balance is never weighed against the accused. And appellate tribunals have the duty to make an independent evaluation of the circumstances. Of course, there is nothing that proscribes the press from reporting events that transpire in the courtroom. But where there is a reasonable likelihood that prejudicial news prior to trial will prevent a fair trial, the judge should continue the case until the threat abates, or transfer it to another county not so permeated with publicity. In addition, sequestration of the jury was something the judge should have raised sua sponte [of his own accord] with counsel. If publicity during the proceedings threatens the fairness of the trial, a new trial should be ordered. But we must remember that reversals are but palliatives; the cure lies in those remedial measures that will prevent the prejudice at its inception. The courts must take such steps by rule and regulation that will protect their processes from prejudicial outside interferences. Neither prosecutors, counsel for defense, the accused, witnesses, court staff nor enforcement officers coming under the jurisdiction of the court should be permitted to frustrate its function. Collaboration between counsel and the press as to information affecting the fairness of a criminal trial is not only subject to regulation, but is highly censurable and worthy of disciplinary measures.

The Public and Press Have a Right to Attend Criminal Trials

Warren Burger

After three mistrials in 1978, the state of Virginia began prosecuting an accused murderer for the fourth time. The lawyers for the defense made a motion to the judge that the proceedings in the fourth trial be closed to the public, and the prosecution did not object.

Reporters did object, however, and appealed the judge's ruling. The case eventually progressed to the Supreme Court in 1980. Even though the criminal trial had long since ended, the Court agreed to decide the question as to whether the Constitution guaranteed the press and public a right of access to criminal trials.

Warren Burger, writing for the majority, indicates that although the Sixth Amendment provides certain guarantees to an accused, the First Amendment cannot be abridged. The public—including the press—must be allowed access to judicial proceedings. Burger was the chief justice of the U.S. Supreme Court from 1969 to 1986.

Here for the first time the Court is asked to decide whether a criminal trial itself may be closed to the public upon the unopposed request of a defendant, without any demonstration that closure is required to protect the defendant's superior right to a fair trial, or that some other overriding consideration requires closure. . . .

People in an open society do not demand infallibility from their institutions, but it is difficult for them to accept what they are prohibited from observing. When a criminal trial is conducted in the open, there is at least an opportunity both

Warren Burger, plurality opinion, *Richmond Newspapers, Inc. v. Virginia,* U.S. Supreme Court, Washington, DC, 1980.

for understanding the system in general and its workings in a particular case: "The educative effect of public attendance is a material advantage. Not only is respect for the law increased and intelligent acquaintance acquired with the methods of government, but a strong confidence in judicial remedies is secured which could never be inspired by a system of secrecy." [John Henry] Wigmore. . . .

Despite the history of criminal trials being presumptively open since long before the Constitution, the State presses its contention that neither the Constitution nor the Bill of Rights contains any provision which by its terms guarantees to the public the right to attend criminal trials. Standing alone, this is correct, but there remains the question whether, absent an explicit provision, the Constitution affords protection against exclusion of the public from criminal trials.

The Prohibition Against Government Interference

The First Amendment, in conjunction with the Fourteenth, prohibits governments from "abridging the freedom of speech, or of the press; or the right of the people peaceably to assemble, and to petition the Government for a redress of grievances." These expressly guaranteed freedoms share a common core purpose of assuring freedom of communication on matters relating to the functioning of government. Plainly it would be difficult to single out any aspect of government of higher concern and importance to the people than the manner in which criminal trials are conducted; . . . recognition of this pervades the centuries-old history of open trials and the opinions of this Court.

The Bill of Rights was enacted against the backdrop of the long history of trials being presumptively open. Public access to trials was then regarded as an important aspect of the process itself. . . . In guaranteeing freedoms such as those of speech and press, the First Amendment can be read as protecting the right of everyone to attend trials so as to give meaning to those explicit guarantees. "The First Amendment goes beyond protection of the press and the self-expression of individuals to prohibit government from limiting the stock of

information from which members of the public may draw."
First National Bank of Boston v. Bellotti (1978). Free speech
carries with it some freedom to listen. "In a variety of con-
texts this Court has referred to a First Amendment right to
'receive information and ideas.'" *Kleindienst v. Mandel*
(1972). What this means in the context of trials is that the
First Amendment guarantees of speech and press, standing
alone, prohibit government from summarily closing courtroom doors which had long been open to the public at the
time that Amendment was adopted. "For the First Amendment does not speak equivocally. . . . It must be taken as a
command of the broadest scope that explicit language, read
in the context of a liberty-loving society, will allow." *Bridges
v. California* (1941). . . .

The right of access to places traditionally open to the public, as criminal trials have long been, may be seen as assured
by the amalgam of the First Amendment guarantees of speech
and press; and their affinity to the right of assembly is not
without relevance. From the outset, the right of assembly was
regarded not only as an independent right but also as a cata-
lyst to augment the free exercise of the other First Amendment rights with which it was deliberately linked by the
draftsmen. "The right of peaceable assembly is a right cog-
nate to those of free speech and free press and is equally fundamental." *De Jonge v. Oregon* (1937). People assemble in
public places not only to speak or to take action, but also to
listen, observe, and learn; indeed, they may "assemble for any
lawful purpose," *Hague v. CIO* (1939) (opinion of Stone, J.).
Subject to the traditional time, place, and manner restrictions, streets, sidewalks, and parks are places traditionally
open, where First Amendment rights may be exercised; a trial
courtroom also is a public place where the people generally—
and representatives of the media—have a right to be present,
and where their presence historically has been thought to enhance the integrity and quality of what takes place.

A Right Does Not Have to Be Explicitly Stated

The State argues that the Constitution nowhere spells out a
guarantee for the right of the public to attend trials, and that

accordingly no such right is protected. . . . But arguments such as the State makes have not precluded recognition of important rights not enumerated. Notwithstanding the appropriate caution against reading into the Constitution rights not explicitly defined, the Court has acknowledged that certain unarticulated rights are implicit in enumerated guarantees. For example, the rights of association and of privacy, the right to be presumed innocent, and the right to be judged by a standard of proof beyond a reasonable doubt in a criminal trial, as well as the right to travel, appear nowhere in the Constitution or Bill of Rights. Yet these important but unarticulated rights have nonetheless been found to share constitutional protection in common with explicit guarantees. . . .

We hold that the right to attend criminal trials is implicit in the guarantees of the First Amendment; without the freedom to attend such trials, which people have exercised for centuries, important aspects of freedom of speech and "of the press could be eviscerated." *Branzburg v. Hayes* (1972) . . . Absent an overriding interest articulated in findings, the trial of a criminal case must be open to the public. Accordingly, the judgment under review is Reversed.

The Pentagon Papers: The Free Press vs. Government Secrecy

Twentieth Century Fund Task Force on the Government and the Press

In 1971 journalists obtained some confidential Pentagon reports—which came to be known as the "Pentagon Papers" —that revealed information about the American involvement in the Vietnam War. The government sued to stop the newspapers from publishing the documents; various major newspapers, including the *New York Times* and the *Washington Post* challenged the order, carrying the case all the way to the Supreme Court. The Court ruled that there was no evidence that publication of the documents posed a threat to national security. Therefore, prohibiting the newspapers from publishing them was an unconstitutional act of prepublication restraint. This case was viewed as a triumph for advocates of a free press.

The following selection was excerpted from a report by the Twentieth Century Fund Task Force on the Government and the Press. Published in 1972, soon after the Supreme Court's ruling on the Pentagon Papers, the report discusses the arguments of the various justices and examines the implications of the case for the press. The authors conclude that government secrecy is detrimental to a free society and that an unfettered press is necessary in order to prevent government misconduct. For these reasons the press must be free to function without fear of prepublication restraint.

Stanley N. Worton, *Freedom of Speech and Press*. Rochelle Park, NJ: Hayden Book Company, Inc., 1975. Copyright © 1975 by Hayden Book Company, Inc. Reproduced by permission.

A fundamental problem of the relationship between governmental power and the press was posed unexpectedly in June of 1971 when the *New York Times*, the *Washington Post* and other newspapers published what has become known as the Pentagon Papers—a group of documents compiled from Defense Department files for a study of the origins of American participation in the Vietnamese war.

The circumstances that surrounded the publication challenged many concepts of the security classification system with which the United States has lived, however uneasily, for a number of decades. The study itself, which had been ordered by Robert S. McNamara while Secretary of Defense, was classified Top Secret. There had been no authorization by any responsible government official for its release to the press. Many of the individual documents, consisting to a great extent of memoranda produced by high officials in the early sixties, were quoted directly by the newspapers without any effort to paraphrase and "fuzz over" their nature. Finally, the sheer bulk of classified material—some 7000 pages—invited a governmental response. The papers could not be ignored, which is and has been the customary official reaction to leaks of individual bits of classified information from Washington.

Initially, the government reaction was to seek injunctions in the Federal courts against further publication of the documents which were being released in serial form. For the purposes of this report, it is unnecessary to trace the various steps of the litigation. The important fact is that on June 30, 1971, the Supreme Court of the United States, by a vote of six to three, dissolved injunctions by lower courts permitting the newspapers to resume publication.

Even though it decided the case, the Court's decision did not resolve the conflict. The Justices were divided even more deeply than the six to three decision indicated, and each member set forth his own views in separate statements. The Court majority concluded that the government did not have the right to prevent the publication of the specific documents in question. But the judicial door seemed pointedly held open for future prosecutions for *having published* the papers. It would be fair to sum up the effect of the decision as one which told the newspapers that they could publish a specific set of documents at their own risk.

For the press as well as for students of the problems of a free society, the outcome did not clarify, once and for all, the relationship between the press and the government. At the heart of the issue was the question of pre-publication restraint—whether there are circumstances under which the government has the right to *prevent* publication. Journalists and commentators have generally assumed that the government has no such right, whatever may be the legal authority to prosecute after the fact for the publication of material offensive to the law. There have been very few cases in the Federal courts bearing upon the issue, and in the Pentagon Papers case the government conceded there had been none which raised the problem in the context of national security.

The Opinions of the Justices

It is worth noting the wide range of attitudes among the Supreme Court Justices on the issue of pre-publication restraint. According to the late Justice [Hugo] Black, "every moment's continuance of the injunctions against these newspapers amounts to a flagrant, indefensible, and continuing violation of the First Amendment;" but according to Justice [John] Harlan, prohibiting prior restraints does not reach "to the point of preventing courts from maintaining the status quo long enough to act responsibly in matters of such national importance as those involved here."

To Justice [William] Douglas the First Amendment left "no room for governmental restraint on the press." By contrast, Justice [Harry] Blackmun argued that "the First Amendment, after all, is only part of an entire Constitution. . . . Each provision of the Constitution is important, and I cannot subscribe to a doctrine of unlimited absolutism for the First Amendment at the cost of downgrading other provisions. . . . What is needed here is a weighing, upon properly developed standards, of the broad right of the press to print and of the very narrow right of the Government to prevent." Justice [William J.] Brennan stated that the First Amendment "tolerates absolutely no prior judicial restraints of the press predicated upon surmise or conjuncture that untoward consequences may result," although he conceded that "there is a single, extremely narrow class of cases (when the nation is at war) in which the First Amendment's ban on prior judicial restraint may be overridden."

Justice [Byron] White held that "prior restraints require an unusually heavy justification under the First Amendment," and concurred in the majority finding because he did not believe the Government had met the test. But Justice [Potter] Stewart commented that "I am convinced that the Executive is correct with respect to some of the documents involved. But I cannot say that disclosure of any of them will surely result in direct, immediate, and irreparable damage to our Nation or its people. That being so, there can under the First Amendment be but one judicial resolution of the issues before us. I join the judgments of the Court." Justice [Thurgood] Marshall noted that Congress has specifically declined to grant the type of authority that the Government sought, adding, "It is not for this Court to fling itself into every breach perceived by some Government official nor is it for this Court to take on itself the burden of enacting law, especially law that Congress has refused to pass."

Chief Justice [Warren] Burger, who dissented from the majority, agreed that there are constitutional limitations on prior restraint. He went on to say that "adherence to this basic constitutional principle, however, does not make this case a simple one. In this case, the imperative of a free and unfettered press comes into collision with another imperative, the effective functioning of a complex modern government and specifically the effective exercise of certain constitutional powers of the executive. Only those who view the First Amendment as an absolute in all circumstances—a view I respect, but reject—can find such a case as this to be simple or easy."

In sum, while basic issues were posed, basic issues were not resolved. The outcome should not be considered a criticism of the Supreme Court. There is good reason to believe that the ends of justice are frequently best served when decisions are made on the narrowest possible grounds, and that sweeping questions of policy are best determined in other arenas. But whatever merit there may be to this view, the fact remains that there is as yet no authoritative concept of whether publication boundaries exist. . . .

In retrospect, it is hardly surprising that the Supreme Court decided the case on relatively narrow grounds or that the public debate was largely irrelevant to the long range issue affecting the press. Whatever may be the venerability of the doctrine of no pre-publication restraint, the publication of the Pentagon Papers raised the issue in a new context which could not have been foreseen by those who wrote the First Amendment. But if the context is new, it does not necessarily invalidate the principles which have governed past conduct. What is clear is that a reexamination is in order. The circumstances of the case required that the litigation be settled within a few weeks, which was hardly an atmosphere conducive to reexamination of underlying issues. From this standpoint, the conduct of the Supreme Court was probably an exercise in wisdom in which the decision did no violence to traditional concepts of freedom of the press while the individual opinions left open the possibility of calmer assessment. . . .

The Political Climate

It . . . is necessary to take into account the general background against which the government's action took place. For at least twenty-five years, the United States has regarded itself as being at "war," whether "hot" or "cold," with an alien ideology. A people who are "at war" have a tendency, rightly or wrongly, to regard the normal processes of democratic life as subordinate to the goal of victory. A plea that certain information must be suppressed to keep it from the hands of an "enemy" or to permit the formation of alliances for "survival" has a much higher degree of acceptability in such an atmosphere than it would in more placid or pacific times.

The psychology of war also fosters a trend of thought which is difficult for a group to discuss calmly. It is based upon the assumption that there are different categories of "rights"—some a matter of "survival" and others a form of "luxury." Under such an assumption, the rights granted to an individual have a tendency to wind up in the second category and those granted to the government in the first. This condition fosters a predilection for very strict enforcement of constitutional guarantees for individual rights in times of serenity when such guarantees are not needed and for forgoing the "luxury" in times of stress.

This type of thinking is more likely to characterize popular debate than judicial confrontation, and no member of the Supreme Court voiced such thoughts in relationship to the Pentagon Papers. But it is only one step removed to conclude that there are certain areas in which some constitutional rights are mutually exclusive, and, therefore, a choice must be made. This consideration *did* influence the thinking of some court members, most notably the Chief Justice [Warren Burger] when he contrasted the "imperative" of an unfettered press with the "imperative" of "effective functioning" of government. His coherent statement can fairly be said to represent the thinking of a large body of responsible men and women who do not regard themselves as in any way opposed to a free press or a free society. It deserves careful analysis.

At first glance, the statement appears unexceptionable. For at least three decades, the nation has accepted the concept that there are "secrets" which would injure the United States if they were revealed to a hostile world. Obviously, it is impossible to publish such secrets in the public press without disclosing them to an enemy. Therefore, the right of a free press is incompatible with government effectiveness, and one must yield to the other. Once this line of reasoning is established, there seems to be little else to discuss than the effectiveness of individual systems for maintaining the necessary secrecy while permitting the maximum degree of press freedom that is possible under such conditions.

It is possible to buttress this line of thought with a number of hypothetical examples which touch off emotional responses that subordinate critical analysis. Usually, they take the form of questions: Would you permit a newspaper to publish the movements of troop ships when enemy submarines are lurking offshore? Would you permit a newspaper to publish codes that would enable an enemy to learn our battle orders? Would you permit newspapers to publish stories that would reveal our weak spots in time of war? Would you permit newspapers to publish our plans of attack and the forces we are going to use?

The short and simple answer is that these questions pose only hypothetical dangers. The practicalities are well illustrated by the system of voluntary censorship set up through government-press cooperation during World War II. Despite occasional slips, usually inadvertent, these voluntary arrangements were entirely adequate to serve military necessity.

But while the dangers inherent in press freedom are largely hypothetical, the threat that would be posed to press freedom by pre-publication restraints is very real. There is historical experience available, because what we now regard as the "free press" emerged only after a long struggle against licensing. The nation's founders knew what they were doing when they wrote the First Amendment. They had learned through bitter experience that no man—no matter how well intentioned—can be entrusted with the power of censorship.

It is apparent that the doctrine of pre-publication restraint can be made effective only through the use of censorship. Usually, the kind of material to which the government objects is not published in serial form. The Pentagon Papers were something of an exception in this respect, and it is unlikely that this kind of exception will occur again. If the government is really worried about its secrets, such fears can be allayed only by inspecting newspaper editions before they hit the streets. Such a practice would open nightmarish prospects for our free institutions. . . .

The Problem with Governmental Secrecy

There is a peculiar characteristic to governmental secrecy that stems from the fact that there is no known method of confining its exercise to limited areas upon which reasonable persons can agree. Because classified security material cannot be examined by the public, the public cannot know whether only material essential to the nation's security is being classified. When people do not know, they tend to become suspicious. These suspicions may not assume a dangerous form when times are good and governmental policies are working well. But at the first setback—and setbacks are inevitable no matter how wise political leaders and their policies may be—the suspicions emerge as a hardened conviction that secrecy has been used to conceal blunders or even fraud and venality. At that point, the declassification and revelation of classified papers does little to restore confidence. An administration that has once resorted to unjustified secrecy can do little to assure a disaffected or skeptical electorate that it is coming clean.

A society without traditions of freedom can handle such disaffection by physical suppression. A free society is a different proposition altogether. Unity cannot be sustained by rifles and police. It requires the confidence of the electorate. Without that confidence, a free government becomes ineffective.

The cost of secrecy is not confined solely to the breeding of suspicion that the government is playing fast and loose with the public trust. It is also a device for cutting off the public debate through which the citizens of a nation prepare themselves for the consequences of great decisions which may mean considerable sacrifice. Nowhere is this better illustrated than in the Pentagon Papers.

The significance of the Pentagon Papers to historians is highly debatable. Whether they shed light on the entry of the United States as a military force in Vietnam is something that cannot, at this point, [in 1972], be determined. But they are unquestionably revealing in terms of the quality of discussion which governed that entry. The most notable characteristic of the passionate debate which was going on within governmental circles is that it took place virtually out of sight and earshot of the public. The American people had only the faintest inklings of the facts and the decisions which were to determine their destiny.

Furthermore, the debate was not conducted under circumstances which fostered calm judgment. Within the government itself, only a relative handful of people were privy to all the facts and options. Yet even this handful were conducting themselves under circumstances which violated all the rules of adversary discussion. They were in a position to write memoranda but could not be certain who would read them or what effect they would have. They did not confront contrary points of view in situations where they could find out what arguments they had to counter. They had no real chance to test their own thinking against others.

In this connection, the Pentagon Papers provide an ironic example of the ultimate futility of secrecy. The papers were put together as a result of Secretary McNamara's request for a study to assist future policy planners in avoiding mistakes made in Vietnam. Once the documents were assembled, fifteen copies were printed and locked up where it was highly unlikely that any future planners would even see them. It is difficult to regard this procedure a satisfactory method for learning from history.

One function of public debate is to test ideas in the marketplace of thought. Another function is to prepare people psychologically for stormy days ahead. In regard to the Vietnamese war, neither function was carried out. On the contrary, all informed discussions took place under a "security" tent. This process left the public in the bewildering position of finding itself involved in a major conflict with no idea of how it got into it or what it was fighting for. Did the United States gain enough advantages from its policy of secrecy to justify the price paid in loss of public confidence? On balance, has the secrecy that was practiced strengthened or weakened the nation?

The members of the Supreme Court addressed themselves to the propriety of the specific classifications of the Pentagon Papers and to the rights of the government to seek injunctive relief. *The task force urges the nation to ponder a broader question—the wisdom of unchecked secrecy itself.*

The task force does not propose the abolition of the security classification system, although we favor a serious study of it by a disinterested group. We are well aware that government of any character will continue to practice secrecy—for good or for bad reasons—in many of its operations. Government officials are human beings, and humans generally assume they have a right to privacy in the conduct of their affairs. It is difficult to convince a person that he does NOT have that right simply because his affairs are in a public domain.

The Importance of a Free Press

Excessive secrecy is inimical in a free society, and should be combated. But we doubt whether a law can be fully adequate to guarantee public inspection of the conduct of public business. *The task force believes that an effective and essential instrument to achieve this end is a free and responsible press—free to investigate; free to interrogate; and free to publish.*

When we weigh the imperative of secrecy against the imperative of an effective government in a free society, we believe that balance is more heavily weighted in favor of the latter.

Admittedly, a free press is a troublesome institution. It can be, and frequently is, arrogant, obnoxious, wrong-headed. We have no illusions as to its reluctance to correct its own faults. But none of its defects is so grave as to justify the abridgment of freedom. Liberty is far too precious to be abandoned out of fear of unpleasant consequences.

Basic to freedom is the right to publish. Obviously, this is a right which entails risks—as does every other right in a free society. The founding fathers did not present the Constitution as a document to insure a painless world. They claimed that it would safeguard liberty, which they considered a fundamental objective.

The task force has neither seen nor heard persuasive evidence that a free press will bring about the downfall of our nation. That latter condition is much more likely to come about through efforts of overly-zealous government officials to protect the public from knowledge of how the public's business is transacted.

But we have seen and heard persuasive evidence that a free government can be effective only when it has the confidence of its citizens. The free press is the most effective instrument known to sustain that confidence. Therefore, a majority of the task force urges that our leaders regard the doctrine of no pre-publication restraint as absolute. No matter what the difficulties, that long-term result will be a stronger and more united nation.

CHAPTER THREE

Current Issues

The Press Does Not Have the Right to Travel with Combat Troops

David B. Sentelle

At the start of the U.S. war against terrorism, during the initial forays into Afghanistan to fight against the al Qaeda terrorist network, the press was clamoring to report on the war. Reporters specifically sought to be "embedded," or integrated, into groups of combat troops as they went into battle. Larry Flynt, publisher of *Hustler* magazine, applied to the Department of Justice for permission for a reporter to travel with military troops as part of the embedding process. When his request was not immediately granted, he filed a lawsuit seeking a declaration of the right of the press to be embedded. David B. Sentelle delivered the decision of the federal court of appeals. He clarified that although the press has a right to information, it does not have a right of access to travel with military units. Sentelle is a judge for the U.S. Court of Appeals for the District of Columbia.

As a threshold matter, it is important to clarify the right appellants seek to protect. In candor, it is not at all clear from appellants' complaint below or briefs in this court precisely what right they believe was violated or contend the courts should vindicate. After some pressing, at oral argument it became clear that they claimed a right, protected under the First Amendment, in their own words, to "go in [to battle] with the military." This right is different from merely a right to cover war. The Government has no rule—at least so far as Flynt has made known to us—that prohibits the

David B. Sentelle, opinion, *Flynt v. Rumsfeld,* U.S. Court of Appeals, Washington, DC, 2004.

media from generally covering war. Although it would be dangerous, a media outlet could presumably purchase a vehicle, equip it with the necessary technical equipment, take it to a region in conflict, and cover events there. . . .

With that distinction made, appellants' claim comes more sharply into focus. They claim that the Constitution guarantees to the media—specifically *Hustler*'s correspondent—the right to travel *with* military units into combat, with all of the accommodations and protections that entails—essentially what is currently known as "embedding." Indeed, at oral argument appellants' counsel stated that the military is "obligated to *accommodate* the press because the press is what informs the electorate as to what our government is doing in war."

The facial challenge is premised on the assertion that there is a First Amendment right for legitimate press representatives to travel with the military, and to be accommodated and otherwise facilitated by the military in their reporting efforts during combat, subject only to reasonable security and safety restrictions. There is nothing we have found in the Constitution, American history, or our case law to support this claim.

To support the position that there is such a constitutional right, appellants first point to cases that discuss the general purposes underlying the First Amendment. . . . These cases, however, say nothing about media access to the U.S. combat units engaged in battle. . . .

Likewise, this Court has held that "freedom of speech [and] of the press do not create any per se right of access to government . . . activities simply because such access might lead to more thorough or better reporting." *JB Pictures, Inc. v. Dep't of Defense* (1996). Appellants admit they face a "dearth of case law concerning press access to battles." From this unenviable position, they ask us to look to *Richmond Newspapers, Inc. v. Virginia* (1980), for guidance.

Richmond Does Not Apply

In *Richmond Newspapers*, a plurality of the Supreme Court held that a constitutional right of public access to criminal trials existed based on a long history of such access in the United States and in England at the time our organic laws were created. According to appellants, *Richmond Newspapers* established that the First Amendment may be interpreted to provide for a right of access to government operations, and that access is not limited to criminal trials. They assert that we must apply a *Richmond Newspapers* analysis to the facts of this case. We disagree.

In *Center for National Security Studies v. Department of Justice* (2003), we held that there was no First Amendment right for plaintiffs to receive the identities of INS [Immigration and Naturalization Service] detainees and material witnesses who were detained in the wake of the September 11 [2001] attacks. Indeed, we made it clear that "neither the Supreme Court nor this Court has applied the *Richmond Newspapers* test outside the context of criminal judicial proceedings or the transcripts of such proceedings." For emphasis, we added that "neither this Court nor the Supreme Court has ever *indicated* that it would" do so (emphasis in original). Instead, we noted that in all areas other than criminal proceedings, the Supreme Court has applied the general rule of *Houchins v. KQED* (1978) (plurality opinion), not the exception of *Richmond Newspapers*. *Houchins* held that the press have no First Amendment right of access to prisons, and in doing so stated that the First Amendment does not "mandate a right of access to government information or sources of information within the government's control." To summarize, neither this Court nor the Supreme Court has ever applied *Richmond Newspapers* outside the context of criminal proceedings, and we will not do so today.

Appellants argue that we did, however, use the *analysis* underlying the *Richmond Newspapers* decision in *JB Pictures, Inc. v. Department of Defense*. In that case, several media and veterans organizations challenged a Department of Defense policy. That policy shifted ceremonies for deceased service members arriving from overseas from Dover Air Force base to locations closer to the service members' homes. It also gave the families of deceased military personnel the authority to limit press access to those ceremonies. Contrary to appellants' assertion, the extent of our *Richmond Newspapers* discussion in that case is contained in one sentence: "[i]t is obvious that military bases do not share the tradition of openness on which the Court relied in striking down restrictions on access to criminal court proceedings in . . . *Richmond Newspapers*." Thus *JB Pictures* not only does not support wholesale adoption of a *Richmond Newspapers* analysis in every case involving requests for access to government activities or information, it rejects such a rule.

Even if we were to apply a *Richmond Newspapers* test, which again, we do not, it would not support appellants' facial challenge to the Directive.[1] As an initial matter, the history of press access to military units is not remotely as extensive as public access to criminal trials. Without going into great historic detail, it is sufficient that in *Richmond Newspapers* the Supreme Court relied on the "unbroken, uncontradicted history" of public access to criminal trials. This includes the time when "our organic laws were adopted." Indeed, ever since "the ancient town meeting form of trial," the "people retained a 'right of visitation' which enabled them to satisfy themselves that justice was in fact being done."

No Historical Right of Access

No comparable history exists to support a right of media access to U.S. military units in combat. The very article cited by appellants for the proposition that media have traditionally had broad access to soldiers in combat does not support this position. Beginning with the American Revolution, war reporting was primarily in the form of private letters from soldiers and official reports that were sent home and published in newspapers. Indeed, the rise of the professional war correspondent did not begin until at least the time of the Civil War. In addition, it is not entirely clear that in any of our early wars the media was actively embedded into units, which is the right appellants seek. In sum, even if we were to attempt a *Richmond Newspapers* analysis and consider the

---

1. Department of Defense Directive 5122.5, the rule that guides decisions regarding media access to combat troops

historical foundations of a right of media access to combat units, appellants' claim would fail miserably.

Even if *Richmond Newspapers* applied in this context, and even if there was a historical basis for media access to troops in combat, the Directive would still not violate the First Amendment. *Richmond Newspapers* expressly stated that "[j]ust as a government may impose reasonable time, place, and manner restrictions" in granting access to public streets, "so may a trial judge . . . impose reasonable limitations on access to a trial." These limitations could be based on the need to maintain a "quiet and orderly setting," or "court-rooms' . . . limited capacity." The Directive appellants challenge is incredibly supportive of media access to the military with only a few limitations. The Directive begins with the command that "open and independent reporting shall be the principal means of coverage of U.S. military operations." It further orders military public affairs officers to "act as liaisons, but not [to] interfere with the reporting process." Additionally, "field commanders should be instructed to permit journalists to ride on military vehicles and aircraft when possible." The restrictions contained in the Directive are few, including: special operations restrictions; limited restrictions on media communications owing to electromagnetic operational security concerns; use of media pools [small numbers of reporters] when the sheer size of interested media is unworkable, such as at the beginning of an operation; and expulsion for members of the media who violate the ground rules. Appellants have offered no reason to conclude that these restrictions are unreasonable. Even if *Richmond Newspapers* did apply, appellants' argument would fail.

The Patriot Act Threatens Freedom of the Press

Reporters Committee for Freedom of the Press

Following the September 11, 2001, terrorist attacks on America, Congress passed the Patriot Act, which President George W. Bush signed into law on October 26, 2001. This law makes it easier for the government to conduct wiretapping and other intelligence gathering in an attempt to prevent terrorist attacks. In the following selection the Reporters Committee for Freedom of the Press describes the law and examines its impact on press freedoms. According to the committee, the law allows the government to require journalists to turn over their notes upon demand, potentially forcing them to reveal the identities of secret sources. In addition, journalists' communications could come under FBI surveillance without their knowledge.

The Reporters Committee for Freedom of the Press is a nonprofit organization whose main mission is to provide free legal assistance to journalists confronted with threats to their First Amendment rights.

The USA PATRIOT Act's impact on newsgathering is still largely unknown nearly two years after Congress rushed to enact the law.

Journalists should be concerned about certain provisions of the law, which grant broad new powers to government agents to investigate terrorism.

Congress enacted the law with little debate just six weeks after the terrorist attacks on the World Trade Center and

The Reporters Committee for Freedom of the Press, "How the War on Terror Affects Access to Information and the Public's Right to Know," www.rcfp.org, September 2003. Copyright © 2003 by The Reporters Committee for Freedom of the Press. Reproduced by permission.

the Pentagon. President Bush signed the USA PATRIOT Act into law on Oct. 26, 2001.

The awkwardly named law—the Uniting and Strengthening America by Providing Appropriate Tools Required to Intercept and Obstruct Terrorism Act of 2001—expands the FBI's ability to obtain records through secret court orders. The law also gives government investigators greater authority to track e-mail and telephone communications and to eavesdrop on those conversations.

Although aimed at trapping terrorists, those provisions of the law could ensnare journalists and compromise their ability to report on the war on terrorism. Journalists should be aware of this law and future amendments and proposals that attempt to expand government surveillance powers and increase secrecy surrounding the government's efforts to combat terrorism.

Secret Court Orders

The USA PATRIOT Act amended certain provisions of Foreign Intelligence Surveillance Act (FISA), thereby expanding the government's ability to conduct surveillance of foreign powers and agents of foreign powers in the United States.

Enacted in 1978, FISA set forth procedures governing foreign intelligence investigations and established a secret court that approves or denies the use of electronic surveillance by the government for foreign intelligence purposes.

The Foreign Intelligence Surveillance Court's 11 judges, who come from different federal circuits, meet twice a month in Washington, D.C., with three judges always available in Washington. The USA PATRIOT Act increased the number of FISA judges to 11 from the previous seven. If the court denies an application for surveillance, the government may appeal to the Foreign Intelligence Surveillance Court of Review, a panel of three federal judges appointed by Chief Justice William Rehnquist.

Secrecy permeates the process of obtaining the court order. The FISA court that issues the surveillance order meets and decides its cases in secret. As a result, the public is left in the dark about the number of FISA search warrants issued against U.S. citizens, who are never informed of the surveillance and are not represented before the court. Not only is the public uninformed, but Congress is kept in the dark about how the FISA court interprets provisions of the USA PATRIOT Act drafted by Congress. The FISA court is not required to reveal its legal opinions, thereby establishing a secret body of case law unprecedented in American jurisprudence. . . .

Under Section 215 of the USA PATRIOT Act, the FBI can seek an order requiring the production of "any tangible thing"—which the law says includes books, records, papers, documents and other items—from anyone for investigations involving foreign intelligence or international terrorism. The person or business receiving the order cannot tell anyone that the FBI sought or obtained the "tangible things."

For journalists, the big question is whether the provision for secret court orders will allow a newsroom search for "any tangible thing" related to a terrorism investigation. Could a government agent use the law to gain access to a reporter's notes and confidential sources?

Theoretically, the USA PATRIOT Act allows a newsroom search. However, another federal law, the Privacy Protection Act of 1980, spells out when newsroom searches are forbidden and the limited exceptions in which they are allowed.

Nothing in the USA PATRIOT Act expressly preempts the Privacy Protection Act.

The Privacy Protection Act states that, "notwithstanding any other law," federal and state officers and employees are prohibited from searching or seizing a journalist's "work product" or "documentary materials" in the journalist's possession. A journalist's work product includes notes and drafts of news stories. Documentary materials include videotapes, audiotapes and computer disks.

Some limited exceptions under the Privacy Protection Act allow the government to search for or seize certain types of national security information, child pornography, evidence that a journalist has committed a crime, or documentary materials that must be immediately seized to prevent death or serious bodily injury.

Documentary materials also may be seized if there is reason to believe that they would be destroyed in the time it took government officers to seek a subpoena. Those materials also can be seized if a court has ordered disclosure, the news organization has refused and all other remedies have been exhausted.

The Privacy Protection Act gives journalists the right to sue the United States or a state government, or federal and state employees, for damages for violating the law. The law also allows journalists to recover attorney's fees and court costs.

The Library Association Complains

While Congress was drafting the USA PATRIOT Act, the American Library Association objected to the potential intrusion into its patrons' personal information, including reading habits and the Web sites they viewed. The group described the law as a threat to patrons' privacy and First Amendment rights. In response, the library association posted guidelines on its Web page advising libraries to avoid creating and retaining unnecessary records.

On Jan. 29, 2003, the library association passed a formal resolution objecting to certain provisions of the USA PATRIOT Act and warned that "the activities of library users, including their use of computers to browse the Web or access e-mail, may be under government surveillance without their knowledge or consent."

Likewise, on Feb. 10, 2003, the American Bar Association adopted a formal resolution that calls for congressional oversight of FISA investigations to ensure that the government is complying with the constitution and limiting improper government intrusion. And the American Civil Liberties Union filed suit challenging the constitutionality of Section 215 in July 2003, arguing among other things that the law violates the First Amendment by allowing the government to easily obtain information about reading habits and expressive activities that will be "chilled" by the threat of a federal investigation, and by imposing a gag order on the third party, such as a library, newspaper or broadcaster, whose records have been taken under such an order.

No one knows exactly how often the USA PATRIOT Act has been used to obtain records, although libraries already have received visits from FBI agents. The Associated Press reported in 2002 that of the 1,020 public libraries surveyed by the Library Research Center at the University of Illinois, 85 said they had been asked by federal or local law enforcement officers for information about patrons related to September 11.

The House Judiciary Committee, which oversees how the Justice Department enforces the USA PATRIOT Act, asked the Justice Department for a more detailed accounting. On June 13, 2002, committee chairman Rep. F. James Sensenbrenner Jr. (R-Wis.) and ranking member Rep. John Conyers Jr. (D-Mich.) sent a list of 50 detailed questions to Attorney General John Ashcroft.

Question 12 asked: "Has the law been used to obtain records from a public library, bookstore or newspaper? If so, how many times?"

The Press Is Not Exempt

In a written response on July 26, 2002, Assistant Attorney General Daniel J. Bryant conceded that newspapers were not exempt from the secret court orders.

"Such an order could conceivably be served on a public library, bookstore, or newspaper, although it is unlikely that such entities maintain those types of records," Bryant wrote.

He declined to state the number of times the government has requested an order or the number of times the FISA court has granted an order. That information is classified, his letter said.

Senator Patrick Leahy (D-Vt.) again sought answers to this question and others after an oversight hearing in July 2002. Of the 93 questions posed by Leahy, 37 remain unanswered.

This type of stonewalling and secrecy was cited in a February 2003 interim report by Senators Leahy, Charles Grassley (R-Iowa), and Arlen Specter (R-Penn.) as "[making] exercise of our oversight responsibilities difficult."

In addition, the interim report found that the refusal of the Department of Justice to disclose the legal opinions and operating rules of the FISA court "contributed to the deficiencies that have hamstrung the implementation of the FISA." Even though members of the Senate Judiciary Committee authored provisions in the USA PATRIOT Act, they were unaware of how the Department of Justice was interpreting these provisions before the FISA court.

In response to this secrecy, Senators Leahy, Grassley and Specter joined together to introduce Senate Bill 436, the Domestic Surveillance Oversight Act of 2003. The bill requires that the rules and procedures of the FISA courts be shared with the U.S. Supreme Court and the Intelligence and Judiciary committees of the Senate and House. In addition, the attorney general must submit an annual public report detailing portions of the applications and opinions of the FISA courts that contain significant legal interpretations of FISA or the constitution. "This type of disclosure . . . will prevent secret case law from developing which interprets both FISA and the Constitution in ways unknown to Congress and the public," said Senator Leahy in a Feb. 25 statement made upon introduction of the bill.

The bill also requires annual reporting on the aggregate number of FISA wiretaps and surveillance orders against Americans and requests for information from libraries.

According to Leahy: "This bill does not in any way diminish the government's powers, but it does allow Congress and the public to monitor their use. We cannot fight terrorism effectively or safely with the lights turned out and with little or no accountability. It is time to harness the power of the sun to enable us to better win this fight."

The bill was referred to the Judiciary Committee, but no action had been taken by late August [2003].

Electronic Surveillance

As long as a reporter is not an "agent of a foreign power," the USA PATRIOT Act does not make it easier for the government to wiretap a reporter's phone. As was the case before the law passed, investigators still must have probable cause to believe a person has committed a crime before they can bug that person's phone.

However, it is now easier for investigators to eavesdrop on a terrorism suspect's telephone calls and e-mail communications with so-called "roving" wiretaps. Because of that change, reporters may run a heightened risk of having their telephone or e-mail conversations with sources intercepted by government agent if those sources are deemed "agents of a foreign power." . . .

What Does This Mean for Journalists?

Lee Tien, senior staff attorney at the Electronic Frontier Foundation, described this scenario:

A reporter contacts a foreign student or a member of a foreign political organization who would meet the definition of "agent of a foreign power" under the Foreign Intelligence Surveillance Act.

Unknown to the reporter, the source is the subject of a roving wiretap authorized under the USA PATRIOT Act.

Because the roving wiretap gives government officials the power to eavesdrop on the suspect's phone and e-mail communications, the government is hearing and recording the reporter's conversation with the source.

As was the case before the USA PATRIOT Act passed, government investigators could not wiretap the reporter's phones and e-mail accounts unless they had probable cause that the reporter had committed or was about to commit a crime.

But by contacting someone who is the target of foreign intelligence surveillance, the reporter might be vulnerable to having a pen register or trap-and-trace device placed on the reporter's phone and e-mail accounts. Remember, the government agent has to certify to a secret court only that the information likely to be obtained would be relevant to an ongoing foreign intelligence investigation. Once approved, the devices give investigators a list of every e-mail address and phone number the reporter is contacting, although not the contents of those communications.

And because all of this goes on in secret, the reporter may never know that his or her communications have been under government surveillance.

How Likely Is This to Happen?

No one knows. In their June 2002 letter to Ashcroft seeking information on how the Justice Department was implementing the USA PATRIOT Act, Reps. Sensenbrenner and Conyers of the House Judiciary Committee asked how many times the department had obtained permission for roving wiretaps, pen registers and trap-and-trace devices. The congressmen did not ask how many times journalists had been caught up in such investigations.

Bryant, the assistant attorney general who responded to the letter, did not provide the information to Sensenbrenner and Conyers. Instead, he wrote them that the information on roving wiretaps was classified; he did not respond at all to the question on pen registers and trap-and-trace devices but indicated that a response would come later.

Reporters do have a measure of protection in the Attorney General's Guidelines for Subpoenaing Members of the News Media, which have been in place since the Nixon administration. Those guidelines, which do not carry the force of law, require that news media subpoenas identify particular relevant information that cannot be obtained any other way. The guidelines also call for negotiations between the Justice Department and the reporter when the agency seeks a subpoena against the news media.

The Bush administration has shown that it will ignore those guidelines if it believes the reporter might have information that could help a criminal investigation.

The Justice Department violated the guidelines in 2001 when it subpoenaed the telephone records of Associated Press reporter John Solomon. The agency was trying to discover the reporter's confidential source for information about a now-closed investigation of Sen. Robert Torricelli (D-N.J.).

Solomon did not learn until late August 2001 about the subpoena, which covered his phone records from May 2 to 7, 2001. The Justice Department did not negotiate with Solomon or his employer, did not say why the reporter's phone records were essential to a criminal investigation, and did not explain why the information could not be obtained any other way.

Also, the Justice Department ignored a provision in the guidelines that allows no more than a 90-day delay in notifying a reporter about a subpoena. The department missed that deadline in the Solomon case.

The Solomon subpoena was issued before September 11 and before Congress enacted the USA PATRIOT Act. But it could be a bellwether event in gauging the willingness of the Bush administration to use journalists as a tool of surveillance.

Reporters Must Have the Right to Keep Sources Confidential

Daniel Scardino

Vanessa Leggett, an aspiring true-crime writer, was research-
ing a murder in Texas. As part of her investigation, she extensively interviewed one of the suspects and spoke with many
other people involved in the investigation. When the prosecution began to face difficulties in building a case, they tried to
enlist Leggett's services as an informant. When she refused,
they subpoenaed her before a grand jury. She refused to reveal her sources and was jailed for contempt. In the following
selection, Daniel Scardino explores the implications of this
case for the press. He concludes that the right of journalists to
keep their sources secret is essential to a free and effective
press. Therefore, the Leggett case is a blow to press freedom.

Scardino is an associate at the law firm Jackson Walker
in Austin, Texas.

When a federal grand jury was convened to investigate
the possibility of filing federal murder charges against
Houstonian Robert Angleton, the city braced itself for another media frenzy. In 1998, Robert Angleton had been acquitted in state court of murdering his wife, socialite Doris
Angleton, who was found shot to death on April 16, 1997, in
her River Oaks home. The state court trial had been a media
circus, replete with a rumored millionaire bookie, his ne'er-
do-well brother, a messy impending divorce, and a jailhouse
confession and suicide.

Daniel Scardino, "Vanessa Leggett Serves Maximum Jail Time, First Amendment–Based
Reporter's Privilege Under Siege," *Communications Lawyer,* vol. 19, Winter 2002. Copyright © 2002 by the American Bar Association. Reproduced by permission.

However, the person who received the most attention was not directly involved in the murder. Vanessa Leggett, a part-time college instructor and aspiring true crime writer, stole the limelight when she refused to turn over to the federal grand jury information that she had gathered during her four-year investigation. On July 19, 2001, Leggett was held in civil contempt as a recalcitrant witness. She went to jail the next day and was not released until January 4, 2002, when the grand jury ended its Angleton investigation without handing down a single indictment.

Leggett was incarcerated longer than any reporter in U.S. history for refusing to disclose research collected in the course of newsgathering. As is usual in states like Texas with no shield laws,[1] neither the district court nor the Fifth Circuit showed compassion for Leggett's professional integrity and loyalty to her confidential sources. She was forced to serve the maximum term for contempt of court, which was the shorter of either the duration of the grand jury investigation or eighteen months.

But the most disconcerting aspect of the Leggett case is that neither court adequately investigated the actions of the U.S. Department of Justice (DOJ) or balanced the interests of the First Amendment against the government's need for Leggett's research. Indeed, there may have been no need for her information at all. On January 8, 2002, four days after Leggett's release, the U.S. attorney empanelled another grand jury to investigate Robert Angleton. It was able to hand down an indictment in sixteen days without subpoenaing Leggett or her records.

Damaging Blow to Reporter's Privilege

Although this scenario has played out between the media and law enforcement agencies many times before, Leggett's contempt citation and the Fifth Circuit's holding represent an especially damaging blow to the reporter's privilege because the court held that the First Amendment did not apply to her case at all. Although the Fifth Circuit settled in dicta [an opinion

---

1. laws that protect journalists from being forced to reveal confidential sources

about a matter not on trial] the issue of whether Leggett was a journalist and thus able to claim the reporter's privilege, it held that the case did not turn on that question. Rather, the Fifth Circuit made the sweeping pronouncement in Leggett's case and an earlier reporter's privilege case that the Constitution does not offer any testimonial or material privilege for reporters in the context of a grand jury or even a criminal proceeding.

The Fifth Circuit's recent decisions are in contrast with those of the U.S. Supreme Court, which held in *Branzburg v. Hayes* that bad-faith grand jury subpoenas intended to disrupt reporters' relationships with their sources violate the First Amendment. In Leggett's case, the court overlooked attempts by law enforcement agencies to use the subpoena power to coerce Leggett to become a confidential informant and turned a blind eye to the policy, embodied in the First Amendment, favoring the dissemination of ideas in furtherance of the public's right to know. The *Branzburg* holding specifically proscribed such law enforcement tactics as violating the First Amendment.

Precisely because Texas has no shield law, Leggett's experience provides a useful context in which to analyze the state of the First Amendment–based reporter's privilege. Leggett has petitioned the U.S. Supreme Court for certiorari [review of the case]; if granted, the Court may fundamentally change the way that most lower courts have applied the First Amendment to subpoenas for the media and their records.

From Ink Slinger to Snitch

Leggett's story began at the arraignment of two suspected murderers and co-conspirators in Houston's Harris County Courthouse. Robert Angleton and his brother Roger were charged with murdering Robert's wife, Doris, after Roger was found in Las Vegas with typewritten notes outlining the murder and a tape recording of two men plotting it. Robert was a Houston millionaire and reputed bookie. Because Robert and Doris's marriage was unraveling, police believed that Robert wanted his wife dead so that she could not reveal the details about his lucrative bookmaking operation during the divorce proceedings.

In the midst of the publicity surrounding the state murder trial, Leggett obtained access to Roger in the Harris County jail through his attorney and recorded over forty hours of interviews. Shortly thereafter, Roger was found dead in his jail cell with a suicide note confessing to the murder and absolving Robert of any involvement in the crime. Eager for evidence to bolster its case against Robert, the Houston district attorney's office subpoenaed Leggett's taped interviews with his now-deceased brother. Leggett initially resisted the subpoena, fearing that her hard work in investigating the crime and getting what she considered an exclusive might be compromised. Eventually, she agreed to comply with the subpoena after the Houston district attorney assured her that (1) only those portions of the interview that were admissible and relevant would be disclosed during the trial, and (2) all copies of the tapes would be returned after the trial. After reviewing the tapes, the district attorney apparently found no new revelations and did not use the tapes at Robert's trial. The trial resulted in an acquittal on August 12, 1998, largely because of the exculpatory portions of the suicide note and a botched Houston police investigation, which revealed that Robert was actually a longtime police informant.

FBI Pressures Leggett

After the acquittal, the Houston prosecutor on the case, Chuck Rosenthal, apparently enlisted his wife, an FBI agent, to pursue Robert on various racketeering, tax evasion, bookmaking, and federal murder-for-hire charges. The FBI began its efforts to seek information from Leggett in July 2000. Although they knew that she was writing a book about the murder and the state trial, federal investigators approached Leggett about working as a confidential informant. The FBI offered Leggett a contract, promising money for her research but stipulating that the FBI would have final say before she could publish her book or otherwise disseminate her material. When Leggett declined, the U.S. attorney handed her a grand jury subpoena on the spot. Leggett complied with the subpoena and appeared before the grand jury on December 7, 2000, where she revealed information but not the names of her sources.

In June 2001, the U.S. attorney served Leggett with a second federal grand jury subpoena that compelled not only her testimony but also the surrender of all research, both originals and copies. Full compliance with that subpoena would have meant that Leggett would have to relinquish all of her research with no guarantee of recovering it. On July 6, 2001, the U.S. District Court for the Southern District of Texas denied Leggett's motion to quash the subpoena as an unconstitutional infringement of the First Amendment. Leggett unsuccessfully argued before Judge Melinda Harmon that the subpoena as issued would prevent her from continuing to work.

On July 18, 2001, the government served Leggett with another, identical subpoena. After a hearing on Leggett's second motion to quash, Judge Harmon issued a contempt order holding that there was absolutely no privilege allowing reporters to withhold any information, confidential or otherwise, in criminal cases. Judge Harmon dismissed as irrelevant any concerns that the DOJ had failed to follow its own guidelines regarding the issuance of subpoenas to the media in its dealings with Leggett.

Writer Goes to Jail

When Leggett went to jail two days later, the media's focus turned from the bizarre murder of Doris Angleton to the even stranger events that resulted in Leggett's incarceration. The press did not unanimously support Leggett's invocation of the reporter's privilege. Although some argued for her release on First Amendment grounds, others argued that the reporter's privilege only protects those associated with major media organizations, not freelancers like Leggett. But most commentators agreed that the DOJ's actions seemed unnecessarily harsh. Why did the DOJ want to deprive Leggett of the ability to work on her book? Wasn't this an unconstitutional prior restraint? Should the DOJ have negotiated with Leggett, as the Houston prosecutor did earlier, so that she could retain control over her material but at the same time give the prosecutors what they wanted?

At least one journalist speculated that the FBI and the U.S. attorney might have wanted to force Leggett to become an informant by threatening to deprive her of her material, ostensibly to prevent disclosure of their own bungled investigation. Leggett's attorney argued that the subpoena was just a fishing expedition. Because Robert Angleton was later indicted by another grand jury without the benefit of Leggett's research, the DOJ apparently did not need her information, lending even more suspicion to its motives. Nevertheless, one thing was clear: with the sheer breadth of media coverage buzzing about the Angleton murder and the dozens of reporters investigating Robert Angleton's past, the DOJ singled out Leggett. She was the only reporter to be subpoenaed in the case.

Some alleged that Leggett attempted to overcome the impossible by claiming the reporter's privilege, impossible because the federal courts, much less the state of Texas, have never recognized an absolute First Amendment–based reporter's privilege. Recent cases suggest that the courts are in the process of limiting the privilege's application even further. Indeed, the history of the reporter's privilege is, for the most part, one of defeat. . . .

Branzburg: Did They or Didn't They?

In *Branzburg v. Hayes*, decided two years after the DOJ guidelines were instituted, the U.S. Supreme Court ruled that a reporter who was working on an ongoing series about the Black Panthers could not refuse to appear before a grand jury that was investigating their allegedly criminal activities. The majority declined to agree with one reporter's assertion of an absolute First Amendment privilege. The Court specifically held that there was no privilege that allowed reporters to refuse to appear before a grand jury or to refuse to answer questions about crimes that they may have witnessed. Citing the public good derived from effective law enforcement and the fact-finding purpose of the grand jury, Justice [Byron] White, writing for the majority, opined that any incidental burden on newsgathering created by compelled testimony before a grand jury was too remote to protect and that no special showing needed to be made before a grand jury could subpoena the press.

However, the majority opinion specifically held that the First Amendment somewhat protected a journalist's cultivation of confidential sources as a form of gathering information. The majority opinion held that "grand jury investigations, if instituted or conducted other than in good faith, would pose wholly different issues for resolution under the First Amendment. . . . We do not expect courts will forget that grand juries must operate within the limits of the First Amendment as well as the Fifth." But this seemingly narrow protection in the context of a grand jury proceeding was supported only by a minority of the Court. Justice [Lewis] Powell, although signing the majority opinion, wrote his own concurrence in which he agreed with the dissenters and advocated a balancing of First Amendment versus law enforcement interests similar to that required by the DOJ guidelines. In terms of the reporter's privilege, Justice Powell's concurrence is the key to *Branzburg:*

> The Court does not hold that newsmen, subpoenaed to testify before a grand jury, are without constitutional rights with respect to the gathering of news or in safeguarding their sources. . . . Indeed, *if the newsman is called upon to give information bearing only a remote and tenuous relationship to the subject of the investigation, or if he has some other reason to believe that his testimony implicates confidential source relationships without a legitimate need of law enforcement,* he will have access to the Court on a motion to quash and an appropriate protective order may be issued. The asserted claim to privilege should be judged on its facts by the striking of a proper balance between freedom of the press and the obligation of all citizens to give relevant testimony with respect to criminal conduct.

Powell, to be absolutely clear, pointed out that "[Justice White's majority opinion does] not hold . . . that state and federal authorities are free to annex the news media as an investigative arm of the government." The fact that he advocated the use of a balancing test even in the context of a grand jury made the narrow language of the majority suspect.

With an unusual majority made up of four justices plus Justice Powell concurring, the actual holding of *Branzburg* has been questioned from the beginning. Justice [Potter] Stewart has called it a case that "rejected a reporter's privilege by a vote of 4 1/2 to 4 1/2."

What Did the Court Mean?

Justice Powell's concurrence went further than the majority's limited holding. Specifically, where the majority indicated that a journalist could only quash a subpoena issued in bad faith, Powell would bar good-faith subpoenas seeking remote and tenuous information. Early commentators were confused by the fact that Powell was the deciding vote and seemingly did not agree with the limited holding of the majority. One even surmised that *Branzburg* was a five-four victory for the press, with Justice Powell plus the four dissenters agreeing on the existence of a qualified reporter's privilege in the context of the grand jury.

Despite the initial confusion, the Powell balancing test, which took into account the relevance and materiality of the information and the ability to otherwise obtain it, eventually became the standard framework for a First Amendment inquiry into media subpoenas. Confusing as it may be, the *Branzburg* decision is the foundation for judicial recognition of a First Amendment–based reporter's privilege. . . .

The Reporter's Dilemma

With the current state of the eroded reporter's privilege, the reporter's dilemma is a palpable one. The ethics of their profession prevent reporters from divulging information obtained in confidence. Reporters are marked as unreliable by sources if they reveal confidences, inhibiting their ability to gather and disseminate accurate and breaking news. If reporters reveal confidential sources, they may be liable in damages to the source for breaking promises of confidentiality. It is a Catch 22: reporters are put in jail if they refuse to reveal their sources and information; if they do reveal their sources, they are monetarily liable for breaching a contract of confidentiality.

Many have dismissed Leggett's lack of cooperation as obstinance or a clever marketing ploy by a savvy young crime writer. But that characterization ignores her significance as a symbol of the press's function as a guardian of democracy. Leggett's investigative efforts to uncover what really happened, including the truth about the Angleton murder, the botched state prosecution, and the ties of Houston's power elite to the crime, represent the true "fourth estate" function of the press in a democracy as the purveyors of systematic transparency. It is precisely this function that most commentators agree the First Amendment was designed to facilitate.

In the context of a grand jury subpoena, the proper inquiry should be whether the actions by federal law enforcement officials to subpoena a reporter are designed to harass and disrupt the reporter's relationship with his or her confidential sources. If the answer is yes, the reporter should not be compelled to testify; if no, the court should balance the competing First Amendment interest with law enforcement's interest in effective prosecution.

In this country, we say we will set ten guilty men free to prevent even one innocent man from going to jail. It is alarming that the courts are not willing to recognize a First Amendment check against prosecutorial misconduct to protect innocent journalists. The deep-rooted prejudices that courts have against the press must sometimes be overcome to protect greater constitutional guarantees. With a proper balance, it is possible for the First and Sixth Amendments to co-exist.

The Origins of the American Bill of Rights

The U.S. Constitution as it was originally created and submitted to the colonies for ratification in 1787 did not include what we now call the Bill of Rights. This omission was the cause of much controversy as Americans debated whether to accept the new Constitution and the new federal government it created. One of the main concerns voiced by opponents of the document was that it lacked a detailed listing of guarantees of certain fundamental individual rights. These critics did not succeed in preventing the Constitution's ratification, but were in large part responsible for the existence of the Bill of Rights.

In 1787 the United States consisted of thirteen former British colonies that had been loosely bound since 1781 by the Articles of Confederation. Since declaring their independence from Great Britain in 1776, the former colonies had established their own colonial governments and constitutions, eight of which had bills of rights written into them. One of the most influential was Virginia's Declaration of Rights. Drafted largely by planter and legislator George Mason in 1776, the seventeen-point document combined philosophical declarations of natural rights with specific limitations on the powers of government. It served as a model for other state constitutions.

The sources for these declarations of rights included English law traditions dating back to the 1215 Magna Carta and the 1689 English Bill of Rights—two historic documents that provided specific legal guarantees of the "true, ancient, and indubitable rights and liberties of the people" of England. Other legal sources included the colonies' original charters, which declared that colonists should have the same "privileges, franchises, and immunities" that they would if they lived in England. The ideas concerning natural rights developed by John Locke and other English philosophers were also influential. Some of these concepts of rights had been cited in the Declaration of Independence to justify the American Revolution.

Unlike the state constitutions, the Articles of Confederation, which served as the national constitution from 1781 to 1788, lacked a bill of rights. Because the national government under the Articles of Confederation had little authority by design, most people believed it posed little threat to civil liberties, rendering a bill of rights unnecessary. However, many influential leaders criticized the very weakness of the national government for creating its own problems; it did not create an effective system for conducting a coherent foreign policy, settling disputes between states, printing money, and coping with internal unrest.

It was against this backdrop that American political leaders convened in Philadelphia in May 1787 with the stated intent to amend the Articles of Confederation. Four months later the Philadelphia Convention, going beyond its original mandate, created a whole new Constitution with a stronger national government. But while the new Constitution included a few provisions protecting certain civil liberties, it did not include any language similar to Virginia's Declaration of Rights. Mason, one of the delegates in Philadelphia, refused to sign the document. He listed his objections in an essay that began:

> There is no Declaration of Rights, and the Laws of the general government being paramount to the laws and constitution of the several States, the Declaration of Rights in the separate States are no security.

Mason's essay was one of hundreds of pamphlets and other writings produced as the colonists debated whether to ratify the new Constitution (nine of the thirteen colonies had to officially ratify the Constitution for it to go into effect). The supporters of the newly drafted Constitution became known as Federalists, while the loosely organized group of opponents were called Antifederalists. Antifederalists opposed the new Constitution for several reasons. They believed the presidency would create a monarchy, Congress would not be truly representative of the people, and state governments would be endangered. However, the argument that proved most effective was that the new document lacked a bill of rights and thereby threatened Americans with the loss of cherished individual liberties. Federalists realized that to gain the support of key states such as New York and Virginia, they needed to pledge to offer amendments to the Constitution that would be added immediately after its ratification. Indeed, it was not until this promise was made that the requisite number of colonies ratified the document. Massachusetts, Virginia, South Carolina, New Hampshire, and New York all included amendment recommendations as part of their decisions to ratify.

One of the leading Federalists, James Madison of Virginia, who was elected to the first Congress to convene under the new Constitution, took the lead in drafting the promised amendments. Under the process provided for in the Constitution, amendments needed to be passed by both the Senate and House of Representatives and then ratified by three-fourths of the states. Madison sifted through the suggestions provided by the states and drew upon the Virginia Declaration of Rights and other state documents in composing twelve amendments, which he introduced to Congress in September 1789. "If they are incorporated into the constitution," he argued in a speech introducing his proposed amendments,

> Independent tribunals of justice will consider themselves in a peculiar manner the guardians of those rights; they will be an impenetrable bulwark against every assumption of power in the legislative or executive; they will be naturally led to resist every encroachment upon rights expressly stipulated for in the constitution by the declaration of rights.

After debate and some changes to Madison's original proposals, Congress approved the twelve amendments and sent them to the states for ratification. Two amendments were not ratified; the remaining ten became known as the Bill of Rights. Their ratification by the states was completed on December 15, 1791.

Supreme Court Cases Involving
Freedom of the Press

1931

Near v. State of Minnesota
A publication printed information that inferred that local law enforcement was under the control of gangsters. The paper was then shut down under a state law. The Supreme Court held that the state could not stop the printing of the publication, but by the time the case had worked its way through the courts, the publisher was bankrupt.

1936

Grosjean v. American Press Co., Inc.
A coalition of nine newspapers challenged the validity of a tax on publications that had a distribution greater than twenty thousand copies. A unanimous Court held that such a tax interfered with press freedom by limiting possible advertising revenue and encouraging lower circulation numbers and therefore violated the First Amendment.

1946

Marsh v. State of Alabama
A Jehovah's Witness attempted to distribute pamphlets in a town that was completely owned by a local company. Operating on the presumption that the town was actually private property, the sheriff arrested her. The Supreme Court held that the private interests of a property owner must be balanced against the individual's First Amendment rights of press and religion. Because the corporation opened the town to the public, the individual rights must be considered more important than the corporation's property rights.

1957

Roth v. United States
In a ruling combining two cases, the Court found that published materials meeting the definition of obscenity are not protected by the First Amendment. Laws against the distribution of such materials were therefore deemed constitutional.

1964

New York Times Co. v. Sullivan
The newspaper published an advertisement that criticized the conduct of a municipal government, but the advertisement included false information. An elected commissioner believed the statements pertained to him and sued for libel. The Supreme Court held that a public official could only obtain damages from a publisher if there was actual malice intended. The press must have the freedom to publish accusations, otherwise free debate would be discouraged.

1966

Sheppard v. Maxwell
The trial of an alleged murderer was covered extensively by the press, calling into question the impartiality of the trial and its jurors. The Supreme Court held that the accused person's right to a fair trial must be balanced against the constitutional guarantee of press freedom and that some limits on the press must be set.

1967

Curtis Publishing Co. v. Butts
A magazine article accused a coach of attempting to fix a college football game, even though the magazine did not verify the story. The coach sued for libel, and the Supreme Court held that the magazine had no defense because the coach was a private individual and not a public figure.

1971

New York Times Co. v. United States
In the infamous Pentagon Papers case, the government tried
to stop the printing of confidential reports on the Vietnam
War obtained by the press. The Supreme Court held that
there was a heavy presumption in favor of the press and that
unless the government could prove that dire consequences
would result, it could not stop the publication.

1972

Branzburg v. Hayes
The Supreme Court considered whether reporters and journalists must respond to grand jury subpoenas and testify
about crimes they may have observed. The Court held that
the freedom of the press guarantee does not create a privilege allowing reporters to choose not to testify before a duly
called grand jury hearing.

1974

Gertz v. Robert Welch, Inc.
A publisher printed false statements about a lawyer involved
in a high-profile case. The lawyer sued for libel and lost because the trial was a public issue. The Supreme Court reversed the decision, saying that the press cannot claim a
constitutional defense for libel against a private individual.

Miami Herald Publishing Co. v. Tornillo
A state law gave political candidates the right to reply free of
charge to newspaper articles that challenged the candidate's
character or official record. The Supreme Court held that the
law was unconstitutional on the grounds that it violated the
right of newspaper editors to publish what they choose.

1975

Bigelow v. Virginia
A newspaper editor from Virginia published an advertisement for a New York abortion clinic and was found guilty of

violating a state law prohibiting the advertising of abortion services. The Supreme Court held that the advertisement deserved First Amendment protection even though it was commercial in nature.

1976

Nebraska Press Assn. v. Stuart

A trial judge, in preparation to hear a murder case and hoping to preserve the defendant's right to a fair trial, granted an order restraining the publication of information regarding the trial, including the events of the preliminary hearing. The Supreme Court held that there was no guarantee that prior restraint in this case would protect the defendant's rights and that alternate measures could have been instituted which would not have denied press freedom.

Time, Inc. v. Firestone

A magazine published inaccurate information about a well-known family's divorce proceedings, and one of the parties sued successfully for defamation. The Supreme Court overturned the ruling on the grounds that the misinformation was not published with malicious intent.

1978

Zurcher v. Stanford Daily

A student newspaper published articles with photographs of an altercation between demonstrators and police. A search warrant was obtained to retrieve photographs and negatives from the newspaper's offices for the purposes of identifying individuals who had assaulted police officers. The newspaper objected, claiming First Amendment rights. The Supreme Court held that because the process of granting search warrants carries inherent safeguards, the newspaper's First Amendment rights were adequately protected and that the search warrants did not violate those rights.

1980

Richmond Newspapers, Inc. v. Virginia
After a number of mistrials, a trial judge ordered that the press be excluded from the fourth attempt at a murder trial. The Supreme Court held that criminal trials have long been open to the public and that the guarantee of the presence of the press helps to ensure that the justice system achieves its objectives.

1982

Globe Newspaper Co. v. Superior Court
For the purpose of protecting the victim's privacy, a Massachusetts law prohibited press and public attendance at criminal trials where the defendant was accused of sexual offenses involving victims under the age of eighteen. The Supreme Court held that the law violated the First Amendment and that the trial judge should be able to evaluate the circumstances on a case-by-case basis to determine if closure is justified.

2001

Bartnicki v. Vopper
A conversation between two union representatives was secretly (and illegally) recorded by a third party during negotiations. The recording found its way into the hands of reporters, and the conversation was published. The Supreme Court, in a narrow decision, held that the release of the information was in the public interest and that the press could not be punished for publishing information that was originally acquired by illegal means.

Books

Lee C. Bollinger, *Images of a Free Press*. Chicago: University of Chicago Press, 1991.

Barbara Dill and Martin London, *At What Price? Libel Law and Freedom of the Press*. New York: Twentieth Century Fund, 1993.

Herbert N. Foerstel, *From Watergate to Monicagate: Ten Controversies in Modern Journalism and Media*. Westport, CT: Greenwood, 2001.

Mark Goodman, *Law of the Student Press*. Arlington, VA: Student Press Law Center, 1994.

Louis E. Ingelhart, *Press Law and Press Freedom for High School Publications*. New York: Greenwood, 1986.

Peter Irons, *May It Please the Court: The First Amendment*. New York: New Press, 1997.

Richard Leone and Greg Anrig, eds., *The War on Our Freedoms: Civil Liberties in an Age of Terrorism*. New York: Century Foundation, 2003.

Leonard W. Levy, *Emergence of a Free Press*. New York: Oxford University Press, 1985.

Anthony Lewis, *Make No Law: The Sullivan Case and the First Amendment*. New York: Random House, 1991.

David Lowenthal, *Present Dangers: Rediscovering the First Amendment*. Dallas: Spence, 2002.

Darien A. McWhirter, *Freedom of Speech, Press, and Assembly*. Phoenix, AZ: Oryx, 1994.

Alexander Meiklejohn, *Free Speech and Its Relation to Self-Government*. New York: Harper, 1948.

E. Joshua Rosenkranz and Bernard Schwartz, eds., *Reason & Passion: Justice Brennan's Enduring Influence*. New York: W.W. Norton, 1997.

Michael Simpson and Marc Abrams, *Law of the Student Press*. Washington, DC: Student Press Law Center, 1985.

Francis Wilkinson, *Essential Liberty: First Amendment Battles for a Free Press*. New York: Columbia University Graduate School of Journalism, 1992.

Web Sites

American Press Institute, www.newspaper.org. This site provides information and resources to journalists, editors, and others involved in the news industry. Its Roundtable section provides articles and commentaries on press issues in society and the marketplace.

Committee to Protect Journalists, www.cpj.org. Established in 1981 and based in New York, the Committee to Protect Journalists describes itself as "an independent, nonprofit organization dedicated to defending press freedom worldwide." The Web site provides information about international issues, including the difficulties faced by foreign correspondents. The site also provides information about the organization's efforts to assist journalists reporting from hostile locations.

The First Amendment Cyber Tribune, www.fact.trib.com. Hosted by Wyoming's *Casper Star Tribune*, this site provides a number of articles, commentaries, links, and historical information on the First Amendment.

First Amendment Project, www.thefirstamendment.org. This site provides educational materials on public records and court access, emphasizing freedom of information. It also operates the California "Anti-SLAPP" resource center, assisting people who have been sued for exercising their constitutional rights, which it terms "strategic lawsuits against public participation."

Legal Information Institute, www.law.cornell.edu. Operated by Cornell Law School, this site provides access to U.S. Supreme Court decisions, lower federal court decisions, acts of Congress, and other legislative materials.

Online Home of the Project for Excellence in Journalism and the Committee of Concerned Journalists, www.jour nalism.org. A resource site for professionals, citizens, students, and teachers, this site includes the "Citizens Bill of Journalism Rights," which emphasizes the role journalists should play in today's society and what the public should expect from journalism professionals, including truthfulness, loyalty to citizens, and giving "voice to the voiceless."

Reporters Committee for Freedom of the Press, www. rcfp.org. Hosted by a nonprofit organization that defends the rights of the press in various court challenges throughout the United States, this site offers reports and briefs on court cases.